the KISSINGER Experience

American Policy in the Middle East

other books by Gil Carl AlRoy

Attitudes Toward Jewish Statehood
in the Middle East

Behind the Middle East Conflict:
The Real Impasse between Arab and Jew

the KISSINGER Experience

American Policy in the Middle East

Gil Carl AlRoy

HORIZON PRESS   New York

Copyright © 1975 by Gil Carl AlRoy

Library of Congress Cataloging in Publication Data

AlRoy, Gil Carl.
The Kissinger experience.

1. United States—Foreign relations—Near East.
2. Near East—Foreign relations—United States.
3. Kissinger, Henry Alfred.
4. Jewish-Arab relations—1967–1973.
5. Israel-Arab War, 1973.
I. Title.
D563.2.U5A76   327.73'056   75-6986
ISBN 0-8180-1604-3

Manufactured in the United States of America

Contents

the KISSINGER Experience

American Policy in the Middle East

part one
Kissinger in Middle Eastern Eyes

1. As Seen by Arabs

To grasp the special impact of Henry Kissinger's Jewishness in the Arab context requires an awareness of the status and vision of Jews in the thirteen-centuries-long Islamic tradition, which is usually lacking in the people of the West and in their communications media. When we see President Sadat, ruler of the largest Arab nation, affectionately embracing and kissing his "Brother Henry," we cannot help but be awed by such an accomplishment by a Jew. The fact is that, while Islam has relegated Jews to subject status, and Muslims find it enormously more difficult to accept the idea of Jewish statehood than Christians in the West, their personal relations with Jews are not usually worse than those of Christians, and sometimes even better. It certainly presents no problem for an Arab leader, particularly when he expects his Jewish guest to produce boon for the Arab cause, as is the case when Sadat receives Kissinger.

The same applies to King Faisal of Saudi Arabia, which was founded by the puritanical Wahhabi sect and bans Jews from its territory. (Another Arab kingdom regarded as pro-American, Jordan, while accepting Jewish visitors, has also insisted on keeping its territory free of Jewish residents.) Faisal banned a French journalist of Jewish descent in the party of the visiting Foreign Minister Jobert, while bestowing on his non-Jewish colleagues presents including literature in praise of Adolf

Hitler.[1] The fact that exception was made for Secretary Kissinger and other Jews in his party reflects the King's appreciation of the greater power represented by the American guest. (The Saudi Arabian government has funded the publication of several hundred thousand copies of an Arab translation of the ridiculous document which, as every literate adult knows, was long ago discredited as a nonsensical fake—the notorious *Protocols of the Elders of Zion*—for distribution throughout the Arab world where that classic anti-semitic tract is a bestseller in several editions, one prepared by a brother of the late President Nasser of Egypt.)

For any Arabic-speaking Westerner the encounter with anti-semitism in the Arab world is immediate and stunning in its virulence. The literary output dealing with Jews is immense and of the quality of the *Protocols*. Whether as books or pamphlets, this anti-semitic literature abounds in stores and street kiosks, and newspapers often feature articles and reports of this genre. A typical item is an interview with King Faisal in a Cairo weekly, which accuses Jews of the ritual murder of French children for the blood they supposedly require for the preparation of the unleavened bread for Passover;[2] or a leading Cairo daily newspaper explaining that the Jewish people are "the enemies of mankind," and praising Hitler's genocide: "History has begun to vindicate the anti-semitic policy of Hitler. The world now understands that Hitler was right and that there was a logical reason for constructing the cremation furnaces, in order to punish those who show such scorn for the principles of humanity, the principles of man, and the faiths and rights of mankind."[3]

A typical academic work reflects the mentality of the educated class. Thus the book of a distinguished author, Mrs. Aisha Abd al-Rahman, (writing under the pen name Bint al-Shati, professor of Arabic literature at Ain Shams University in Cairo), a synopsis of which was published in the literary supplement of *Al-Ahram* (June 2, 1967), the Arab world's most prestigious newspaper. According to her, the history of mankind revolves around a running struggle of all humanity trying to rid itself of the poison of Judaism. All history is divided into several rounds of one and the same battle between the antagonists; the war has been raging from the days of the Babylonians to the present, and from Mesopotamia and the Nile Valley to Germany and beyond. The task of modern Arabs is finally to accomplish the ends of all history and humanity, in exterminating this evil. Her design includes both leftist theories of the Jewish state as the tool and running dog of imperialism and the more traditional allusions to deep-rooted cowardice and depravity inherent in Jewish nature. This characterization of the Jews is repeatedly proclaimed by religious authorities. The leading Muslim theologians summoned under government auspices to Cairo termed them "enemies of God" and "enemies of humanity," and demanded that the world be cleansed of them, whose wickedness and perversity was said to be inherent and incurable, unless subjected by force under the heel of Muslims.[4] And characteristic of the prevailing atmosphere, though on a lighter note, is the rejection by Arabs of foreign films showing Jews in a favorable light. The Libyans thus refused to accept the Ben Casey television series because they thought the hero was Jewish and took it only after they were assured that it was an Italo-American actor playing the part of an Irish-American.[5]

Arab spokesmen in the West are anxious to explain that they distinguish between Jews and Zionists. The irony in this is twofold: to begin with, Arabs themselves invariably use these terms interchangeably; the distinction itself is a left-handed compliment, for it means that only the Jews, unlike all other people, are not entitled to national independence. Zionism, which is Jewish nationalism, is therefore the perverse version of Judaism.

The other standard way of explaining away this avalanche of anti-semitism is to argue that, since Arabs are themselves semites, they cannot possibly be anti-semites. There is both spurious reasoning and unintended irony in this common claim, since it is based on the racist pseudo-scientific theories of the last century which spoke of superior Aryans and so on. In fact, Jews and Arabs are fellow-semites only in that both speak semitic languages and thus share 'no more common identity than Bengalis and Englishmen, who also speak related languages. Moreover, anti-semitism has never been concerned with anyone but Jews. As Bernard Lewis pointed out: "The Nazis, who may be accepted as the most authoritative exponents of anti-Semitism, made it quite clear that their hostility was limited to Jews only, and did not include the other so-called Semitic people. On the contrary, the Nazis found and still find no difficulty in simultaneously hating Jews and courting Arabs; they made a considerable and on the whole successful effort to cultivate the Arabs, and won the friendship and support of many Arab leaders, including some who still hold high office."[6]

What is particularly disturbing is that anti-semitism is not mere rhetoric, but comes out of genuine attitudes in even the educated class in the Arab world, as both impressionistic and rigorous studies reveal. The Prothro-Melikan study of university students from various Arab countries showed that Jews (and Negroes) were the most definitely stereotyped and the least favorably regarded among all thirteen national groups surveyed.[7] A more recent survey for this writer by a researcher with close ties to his informants disclosed that even among upper-class Arabs serving in the United States stereotypical misperceptions of Jews as of the "merchant" type and other varieties are very common. But in private conversation these men usually disclaim any hostility and even make ingratiating statements. Nadav Safran reported upon returning from Cairo late in 1974, that he had just such an experience with an Egyptian notable who knew of both his Jewishness and his position in America as a Harvard professor. But in the street, a taxi driver vented his hostility toward Jews quite readily to him; and he could not miss the anti-semitic literature on the stands.[8]

It will probably startle Americans to discover that Sadat, the leader they believe is turning his people away from Nasser's policy of confrontation with Israel, was among the most active pro-Nazi militants during Hitler's heyday and later publicly justified the deeds of the Führer.[9] But that does not prevent him from receiving Jews and perhaps even liking them. Many men in the Arab world see little inconsistency between this—even marrying Jewish women—and admiration for Hitler. As they see it there is little wrong with Jews who know their place; it is in the unnatural presumption to dominion, as in Jewish statehood, that an ancient accursed and vicious streak of the Jews— as the holy Muslim scriptures warn—manifests itself. Arabs see Hitler as having struggled against the accursed side of Judaism and indeed often express disbelief that he exterminated so many Jews.

It is in this context that Kissinger's reception in the Arab world, which has awed even the Washington elite, assumes a more understandable dimension. The awe would diminish if one also knew something of interpersonal relations in the Arab world, where often effusive behavior may disguise a hostile relationship. While marveling over Kissinger's achievement in getting Sadat so fast on a "Dear Henry" basis, the press forgot to mention that the previous Secretary of State, William Rogers, was also immediately greeted as "Dear Bill" upon his arrival in Cairo, at a time when America was denounced there and in other Arab capitals as the epitome of evil.

Not only is there no difficulty to overcome in a diplomatic mission by someone of Jewish descent seen as enhancing the Arab cause, there is a fascination in it. While demeaning them in terms of politics and power, Muslims have long suspected the likelihood among Jews of miraculous, supernatural powers; even now Jewish physicians are preferred to others for their special touch or grace. (On the other hand, the same belief in Jewish magic inclines Arabs toward accepting spurious theories of Jewish world domination, as in the fake *Protocols* and other comparably reliable tracts.) It is thus right in a profound sense that a Jew—"Doctor Henry," Sadat calls him—should come to heal the Arabs' pain.

Sadat's exhilaration with Kissinger reflects also gratification with the astuteness of his strategy, which had identified America as the only power capable of forcing Israel to submit to Arab terms (on this the Arab consensus is overwhelming) and Kissinger as perhaps the only American statesman ready and able to make that potential reality (on this there is less than full agreement among Arabs). It was Sadat who asked President Nixon in the spring of 1972 to assign Kissinger to the Arab-Israeli impasse, where movement, in his conception as well as that of virtually all participants in international diplomacy—including the American State Department—could come in the last resort only by pushing Israel. According to Sadat's confidant Mohammed Hassanein Haikal, writing in Beirut's *Al-Anwar* on December 29, 1973, Sadat's interest in Kissinger rose sharply early in 1971 as soon as it appeared that the Israelis had successfully resisted the pressure to relinquish the territorial gains of 1967. One man who then sought to impress the Egyptian leaders with the imperative need for them to befriend Kissinger was Donald Kendall, chairman of the board of Pepsi-Cola Company and a close friend of Richard Nixon. Haikal recounted Kendall's May, 1971, visit to Cairo, and citing correspondence with Kendall and others, shows the American engaging in a whirlwind campaign to bring Kissinger and the Arabs together in order to break Israel's resistance to foreign pressure and "for serving Arab interests in general." (Kendall later appeared as Kissinger's ally in the struggle against the forces that sought to promote the emigration of Soviet Jews in return for trade concessions to Moscow.) What recommended Kissinger for the job, where so many, including William Rogers and Gunnar Jarring, had failed, was above all his record in Vietnam and elsewhere and his reputed abhorrence of personal failure. Sadat and other Arab leaders often expressed their admiration for his attraction to power and his manipulation of it, and he was clearly their first choice when Rogers finally went, in August, 1973.[10]

So widespread was the sense of Sadat's "waiting" for Kissinger that it was even suspected that the timing of the Arab attack on Israel so soon after the latter's assumption of his new office was influenced by it.[11] Sadat's exposition of the grave events of October and after portrays the Arabs as alone forcing a turnabout in the regional and global power balances; not only not coordinating either signals or strategy with the superpowers, but actually compelling both America and Israel to heed the Arabs' will, by the power of their armies and their oil. He had the satisfaction of repeatedly announcing it publicly to the visiting President Nixon without even a hint of displeasure; Kissinger had previously not merely endorsed this flattering image, but actually let it be known that the Arabs were even so selling themselves short, both in talks with Arab and Jewish leaders.

But on many occasions Arab sources identified the Secretary as a decisive factor in the turn of events in their favor, and Sadat has attributed to him "particular" credit for it.[12] Following repeated expressions of anxiety about the Nixon-Kissinger team in the Watergate scandal, Arab spokesmen voiced confidence when President Ford retained Kissinger. While this anxious attachment to a particular policy-maker has been explained here as merely a matter of personal preference in dealing with an America whose policy, being really impersonal, remains the same regardless of the identity of its policy-makers, the Arabs seem to think otherwise. This is not only because the marked concreteness in their culture inclines them strongly toward the particular and specific rather than the abstract; but also because their experience with American power indicates to them a much greater range of policies than most Americans suspect. It may be true that Kissinger was pursuing the policy of his predecessor, Rogers—to obtain virtually total Israeli withdrawal from lands acquired in the 1967 war—but Rogers could not implement the Rogers Plan, while Kissinger seemed indeed to be doing it already. Consider the conduct of the Nixon and Johnson administrations in "their" Middle East wars: in 1967 Washington insulated the war from superpower interference, allowing Israel to overwhelm the Arabs; in 1973, by contrast, it joined Moscow to force a halt to the same denouement, already progressing fast. As an Indian officer saw it from the Arab perspective, Washington acted this time with a view "that it would probably be best for the Israelis to suffer a limited defeat."[13] The difference is enormous.

The guns were not yet silent when Kissinger descended on the Middle East in a mission unprecedented in intensity of energy, travel, media coverage, and not least perhaps in its character. For while it is true that the Eisenhower-Dulles team saved Nasser from the consequences of military defeat in 1956, it did not go beyond restoration of the status quo ante bellum. Kissinger's exertions in this case quickly restored to the Arabs all their territorial losses in a war they themselves had started, as well as other areas they had not held before the war. To grasp Sadat's elation over the "disengagement" secured by Kissinger in January of 1974, one must try to see, from his corner, the advantages he obtains: freedom for his Third Army that had been in a trap; the whole Israeli bridgehead on the west bank of the Suez Canal, pointed at Cairo; the whole length of the west bank of the Canal to a depth of some ten miles—all this from being on the brink of a disaster prevented by Kissinger. He remains free to rattle his rockets against Israel's cities, to intervene militarily on other fronts, and to roll over the United Nations buffer force in the Sinai with virtual immunity, which is almost unthinkable for Israel, given her isolated international position. This is only the beginning. "Disengagement" means similarly one-sided deals for Syria and probably also Jordan, and other shibboleths will designate further recovery of lost territory until Israel is pushed back to the armistice lines of 1949 (in effect at the start of the June War of 1967). Then Israel must be made to satisfy the "national" and "legitimate" rights of the Palestinian people—a notion full of ambiguity for Westerners and pregnant with catastrophic connotations in the Arab context.

Meanwhile Egypt, more than other Arab states, enjoys special affection and other bounty from the cornucopia of America —without having to forgo either the political or military support of Russia, which, despite some expression of displeasure at the rapprochement with Washington, persists in competing for Arab favor, in Egypt as elsewhere. Visitors to Cairo return with tales of the exultation of Egyptians at the American manna showering them. The United States Navy helps unblock the Suez Canal; one quarter of a billion dollars has been set as a start in aid and 100,000 tons of wheat to feed Egypt's teeming population. Egypt reportedly asked for three quarters of a billion dollars worth of products. Sadat announced his intention to present a bill for two billion dollars to Washington for the petroleum lost to Egypt during Israel's occupation of the Sinai, while Egypt's ally, Saudi Arabia, had collected such an immense toll for oil from America and other nations that their economies have faced crisis. Syria was to get large quantities of wheat and rice and other aid.

And perhaps the greatest gift is that of nuclear technology from America to Egypt, as stunning to many Americans as it is exciting to the whole Arab world. There is an air of anticipation that, with the ultimate weapon inevitably and soon in their hands, the Arabs will make final disposition of the problem that has tormented them for nearly half a century. This conviction is stated publicly in Cairo's *Al-Ahram* (June 6, 1974) and a cartoon in that influential newspaper epitomizes the spirit pervading the Arab press, as it shows a line of figures queuing up before a guillotine, the inscriptions on the figures reading in this order: "Moshe Dayan," "the Government of Israel," "the Israeli political system," and finally "Zionism" itself.

2. As Seen by Israelis

Much as Washington may desire Arabs and Israelis not to treat their quest for American support as a zero-sum game, they almost invariably do. American overtures to the Arab world, like similar moves in previous years, did not fail to cause great anxiety in Israel. Despite the impression conveyed by the Administration and the press that the present "breakthrough" is somehow unprecedented and historic, like the opening to Communist China, the Israeli discontent had begun earlier, with the assumption of office by Henry Kissinger. For their side, like that of the Arabs, sensed in this much more than a change of incumbents, both because of the Secretary's reputation and his Jewishness.

That the Jewishness of Kissinger had relevance to his involvement in the Arab-Israeli dispute was indisputable, as evident anxiety among Jews in Israel and elsewhere accompanied his assumption of the senior position in the Cabinet. The trouble was that the usual discourse on this matter tended to raise the wrong questions—whether he would favor Jewish interests over the national interest (which betrays ignorance of Jewish attitudes), and whether he would be unacceptable to the Arabs (which betrays ignorance of *their* attitudes).

Actually, Jewish anxiety arises from the fact that Jews in high office in the gentile world have all too often felt irresistible pressures to prove their loyalty to their benefactors, sometimes by acting egregiously against Jewish interests. While a not insignificant number of Jews have occupied positions in the government of important nations in the last several decades, they have proved remarkably negative in the momentous concerns of the Jewish people in that period. It is characteristic that, in the struggle for the Balfour Declaration of 1917, which greatly raised the international status of the Zionist movement, the highest British official of Jewish descent, Edwin Montagu, was among the staunchest opponents of that document. In the United States, where Jews felt more secure than elsewhere in identifying with Jewish causes, this has more often been the case with those of Eastern European background than with Jews of German background (like Kissinger's). The latter's attitude has been described as "a blend of defensiveness, apology, and anxiety—a condition expressed by the Yiddish word *tsitter*, whose very sound suggested trembling and uncertainty."[1] German Jews were known to the East European Jews as "Yahudim," a somewhat derisive term signifying economic success, acculturation, and anxiety lest one's Americanism be compromised or questioned because of one's Jewish assertiveness. Their reaction to Zionism was negative, almost violently so, but tending more recently toward acquiescence and even acceptance. In the view of many American Jews, Henry Kissinger fitted this syndrome sufficiently to cause them discomfort. A book published a year before described him as constantly trying to suppress identification with Jews.[2]

One of the few unequivocal patterns emerging from the mass of interviews by *The New York Post* staff for Blumenfeld's *Henry Kissinger*, is just this "Yahudi" attitude in almost exaggerated form. Thus Henry Kissinger discarded his Orthodox Jewish religion as a very young man and seemed to have held on to it earlier only for his parents' sake. He anxiously shunned associations with Jewishness as an adult. On the one occasion when, as a Harvard professor, he did address a group identified with work in Israel, it was because his mother had asked him, and when he came, he managed not to mention Israel at all in his address. At the same time he strove strongly to appear as more American than more conventional Americans. His Harvard teacher, Carl Friedrich, recalls that Kissinger frequently clashed with him over his support of Zionism, which Kissinger denounced as harmful for America. Fritz Kraemer, the man who knows Kissinger as few others do, having "discovered" him in military service and directed his career toward intelligence work and Harvard, expressed his conviction that Kissinger had no interest in the fate of the three million Jews in Israel, even if they were to perish as a consequence of his policies. When Kissinger took the oath of office, as Secretary of State, he made emphatic assertions of loyalty and gratitude for his appointment, citing his background. Although the Old Testament was available, he used the New Testament instead and did it on the Sabbath, to boot. Among his first acts of office was an extraordinary order to Jewish employees of the State Department to work on their High Holidays.

By curious coincidence the Israelis were just then immersed in the Kreisky Affair, a matter in which they felt that the Jewish background of the Austrian Premier had impelled him to accommodate the Palestinian *fedayeen* so greatly as to bestow on them unprecedented triumph as he bowed to their demand that Austria cease assisting the flow of Soviet Jewish immigration to Israel with the elaborate halfway house facilities at Schönau Castle. It was somehow fitting to the Jewish tradition that the only European government to submit to policy dictation by terrorists from the Middle East was headed by a Jew. "We all know what Kreisky is," said a senior Israeli official, "an uneasy Jew, especially uneasy as a Jewish politician who made it to the top in a country with a long history of vicious anti-Semitism."[3] For his part, Bruno Kreisky evidenced a need to vindicate his lifelong rejection of Jewish nationalism in favor of Austrian socialism; his rejection of the Israeli appeal from his pro-Arab decision was gratuitiously unpleasant. "He didn't even offer me a glass of water," said Mrs. Meir after their acrimonious meeting in Vienna. (The police code word for her visit was—incredibly— *Schinkensemmel*, or ham sandwich.)

The new Secretary's reputation was only too soon confirmed by events that precipitously engulfed Israel. Israelis were
just starting to face his approach when they had to turn their
attention to reported peace plans of the new Secretary, only to
be startled by the boldness of his first overtures to the Arab
world; and came under massive attack by Arab armies on two
fronts. This unnerving loss of control and mere reaction to
others' initiatives is a pattern that continues to mark their policy
in the Kissinger era, and many Israelis are sure that the coincidence is not accidental.

Like the Arabs, the Israelis also noted that war between
them, under the new dispensation, was a much different experience from the previous one, under Lyndon Johnson. While Israel reeled under a gigantic onslaught, fueled by ships and planes
from Soviet stores, her American connection had suddenly
waned. The man reputed to succeed where none could, to
bring off the impossible, to move mountains, now startlingly
declared himself unable even to effect the vital rearmament of
Israel's forces. For many days, as the bloodmills of the battle-
fronts churned and suffering mounted, the seeming impotence
of this powerful man lingered—failed, he said, by Washington
bureaucrats. But when newly supplied Israeli forces turned the
tide toward accelerating demolition of Arab armies, the Secretary just as curiously regained his reputed vitality and power.
Suddenly, nothing could keep him from halting the Israelis and
ensuring the welfare of the Egyptian army they had trapped.
Facing the press, as the war raged, the Secretary could not bring
himself to criticize the Arab attack and strained to put the best
possible construction on openly incendiary Soviet behavior. As
it died down, he raced into the embrace of Sadat. The sense of
all this suddenly registered in Israel's popular mood as despondency. (The American press soon informed us of this drastic
change, but falsely attributed it to high casualties among Israel's
soldiers, public awareness of which came only later, to further
deepen despondency.)

Kissinger's involvement in the Middle East conflict was
accompanied by a series of publicized remarks which could not

fail to offend Jewish sensitivities. Thus his reported denunciation of Golda Meir's "Jewish ghetto" conviction that the world is against Israel: "As she sees the Mideast showdown, according to Kissinger, most nations have bowed cravenly to Arab oil blackmail. She compares this to the British and French backdown at Munich to Adolf Hitler's blackmail. She recalls bitterly that Britain's present foreign secretary, Sir Alec Douglas-Home, as a young parliamentary aide, accompanied Neville Chamberlain to the Munich conference. . . ."[4] (He did—as the young Lord Dunglass.)

This attitude found expression in official policy, most notably in an act relating to the terror strike at Qiryat Shmona, the slaughter of eighteen Jews there deeply stirring American Jewry. As is usual, the United Nations Security Council moved to condemn Israel for a retaliatory raid across the Lebanese border. Whereas the United States previously in such cases always expressed displeasure at the patent one-sidedness of these censures and insisted on at least mention of the provocation for acquiescing in their passage, this time it actively supported a censure resolution from which reference to Qiryat Shmona had been deleted. As it turned out, the United States had itself made the deletion, as reported by Western European diplomats at the United Nations. "According to these accounts, a draft text, agreed to by Britain, France, Austria and Australia, had a reference to Qiryat Shmona. The draft was discussed in Washington last Friday when Secretary Kissinger met with the Lebanese Foreign Minister, Fuad Naffah. 'All I know is that the text came back without a reference to Qiryat Shmona,' said one European. 'If it was satisfactory to the Americans, we did not want to be more Papal than the Pope.' "[5]

Other Kissinger remarks were intimidating, touching on characteristically Jewish fears. One recurrent theme in his expositions was the doom of the renewed Jewish Commonwealth. In a widely publicized meeting on December 6, 1973, with several Jewish intellectuals, who had hoped to be reassured by the Secretary, he put across the idea that Israel "has had it"; the Jewish state was sinking fast militarily, diplomatically and in its standing in Congress and the nation's opinion—unless it threw itself completely on his diplomacy and Arab good will. Variations on this theme were reported in other places.[6] Kissinger also fanned fears of widespread anti-semitic outbreaks. Through James Reston, whose columns served as his platform, he warned that, unless America's Jews and Israel acquiesced in his Middle East policy, the American people and others would blame them for their misfortunes wrought by the Arab oil embargo. (American public opinion, as measured in surveys, actually belied this judgment.) American Jews were greatly disconcerted by the Secretary's intimacy with the then Senator Fulbright, whom they ranked lowest in concern for their aspirations among all his peers.

Most troubling was the character of Kissinger's dealings with Jewish leaders, both in the United States and in Israel. Because of the nature of interaction at the top, awareness of this attitude was at first limited to few individuals and those involved were understandably reluctant to advertise it. But some reports soon disclosed a pattern in Kissinger's handling of Jewish leaders. A former official in Israel's Ministry of Foreign Affairs, said of Jerusalem's leaders' experience with Kissinger, that they can be genuinely touched by his recollections from a terrible past, as a Jewish youth in Nazi Germany, only to be stunned to discover, after his departure, that he has unilaterally altered the text of an agreement worked out during his visit.

Arab sources close to the disengagement negotiations were saying that Kissinger's mediation was in effect a bargaining with the Arab side, in the expectation that he would then bring the Israelis around to acquiesce in the agreement.[7] As was widely reported in the American press, the fear that, despite his denials, Kissinger had already concluded *their* agreements with the Arabs, caused the Israelis nightmares and lingers with them still. When he allowed them a glimpse of his vision of the Middle East upon a successful conclusion of the diplomatic process he had initiated, as in the December 6, 1973, meeting with Jewish intellectuals, it looked pretty much as though it would involve Israel's capitulation to current Arab terms for settlement. The

rulers of Egypt and Syria have repeatedly claimed that Kissinger's vision of a settlement is very close to their own. The
persistence of Kissinger's approach to Israel has more recently so
troubled her leaders, that they overcame their strong reticence
about appearing at odds with him. In one case, the Secretary
announced at a Washington news conference an invitation to
Premier Rabin to visit the capital, although the matter had not
been resolved between the two countries; such procedure, Israeli officials said, was "unheard of" in international relations,
and press comment in Tel Aviv likened the Secretary to a Mafia
boss.[8] The unilateral choice of time placed the Israelis at a disadvantage at the very start of a new round of negotiations with
Arab states. Kissinger had used other tactics during the earlier
disengagement negotiations in order to put the Israelis at a
similar disadvantage, having to expose first their bargaining
stance to the Arabs. The Secretary has shown condescension
toward the Jewish state in denying it courtesies extended to
Arab states; for example, personally greeting Arab foreign min-
isters in Washington, but sending a subordinate to receive the
Israeli minister.[9]

Although there are nuances in Israeli attitudes toward Kissinger, a sense of anxiety and distrust seems common, apparent
even in the small minority of so-called "dovish" elements, who
come as close to being a Kissinger party as any Jewish group
can in Israel's present emotional and intellectual climate. It is
characterized by a less pessimistic evaluation of chances for
peace than in the rest of the country and also by visions of a
small Israel insulated from power politics by diplomatic arrangements. This inclines them toward Kissinger—among whose
mentors on Middle East affairs reportedly was Nahum Gold-
mann, perhaps the most "dovish" of Zionist leaders—but other
fears persist. Thus Shulamit Aloni, whose recent appointment
to the cabinet has strengthened this faction, on the Geneva conference arranged by Kissinger: "We have to go to Geneva," she
said, "but we don't want Kissinger to bring to the Middle East
the kind of peace he brought to Vietnam. There is no peace in
Vietnam."[10]

Since "dovish" opinion is greatly over-represented in the

Israeli government and among the more articulate segments of the population, such as academics and journalists, especially those among them who address foreign publics, the latter obtain but faint signals of the actual state of affairs. Stringent political considerations further extend this circumstance, since the heightened dependence on the United States greatly restrains the Israeli government from venting discontent with it. The fact that Secretary Kissinger appears more secure in American public support in respect to the Middle East than in any other area suggests to Jerusalem that fighting him now may be futile, and possibly counterproductive. They cooperate with him simply because they must, while trying to put the best publicity face on it, resolved to fight him if pressed beyond positions they can live with, some of them trusting that moment never arrives.

In the aftermath of the disengagement agreements with Egypt and Syria, the national sense of relief over the return of tens of thousands of soldiers to their homes and the repatriation of prisoners of war and the return of some of the fallen for burial in Israel temporarily overshadowed the fear of Kissinger. By mid-summer, however, the opinion polls increasingly indicated sharp falls in public satisfaction with his performance, the drop being especially marked among the Western Jews, while the Jews from Oriental countries, much like the Arabs whose culture they substantially share, still tended to attribute magic qualities to him. A conspicuously critical view of Kissinger crystallized in the fall of 1974, when one of the largest demonstrations outside the Prime Minister's offices urged his exalted American guest to "go home," and "burn oil, not Jews."[11]

Marilyn Berger, who accompanied Kissinger, wrote: "The No. 1 question in Israel was: Could Kissinger be trusted? How could he be, when he had to appease the Arabs because they had the oil and he was concerned about the potential devastating effects of the oil-price crisis on the Western world? And wouldn't he sell out Israel if it meant the avoidance of nuclear war? Only a Jewish Secretary of State could sell out the Jewish state. Look at what he had done during the October War. Wasn't it Kissinger who had stopped the Israeli advance, who had agreed to a ceasefire when the Russians demanded it, just to set the stage for his own brand of diplomacy, which required a stalemate on the battlefield? Didn't some reports indicate that Kissinger had actually held off on American arms deliveries to Israel just long enough to make a clean, lightning victory impossible? Could this man be an honest broker?"[12]

But there lingers, on the other hand, the incredulity that a Jew, indeed one who has experienced some of Hitler's persecution of Jews and lost some relatives to his gas chambers, would be able to sell out the Jewish state. It would seem like an utterly insane notion, particularly to Jews living in the Jewish state. Thus deepest anxiety is tinged with disbelief, bordering in some on despair for their sanity. Kissinger, himself, who Israeli leaders have said likes to appeal for their confidence by citing his refugee-from-holocaust background, was greatly annoyed when they actually took him to the memorial to holocaust victims. When one Israeli once made a casual reference to his Jewishness at a public reception in Jerusalem, Kissinger seemed so disturbed that those present feared he would leave the room.

Though harboring few illusions about Kissinger, some influential Israelis fear that he might be replaced in this unfortunate period in America's life by someone treacherous and less intelligent. And some also harbor fears of an anti-semitic backlash in America from any popular discontent with a "Jewish" Secretary of State.

As for American Jewry, the largest and most influential Jewish community in the Diaspora, it hovers in a state of painful confusion, mixed emotions and contradictory signals. American Jews suffer tension between spontaneous "gut" feelings of distrust and fear and the contradictory pull of the national folklore about the miraculous Secretary dispensed by the media they consume along with their Gentile countrymen. The official Jewish leadership, many of whose members harbor grave anxieties privately, follows the line laid down in Jerusalem. (It is neither as formidable a force in American policy-making as the media and Arab sympathizers pretend, nor is it as independent of Jerusalem as it pretends.) The "Jewish Establishment" has sought to play down evidence of popular anxiety and has lent itself to attempts from Washington to silence articulate critics of Secretary Kissinger.

Thus it fell to Irving Howe, a literary critic, both strange to this officialdom and unenthusiastic about quite a few aspects of Israeli life and politics, to speak of Jewish anguish in public: "There are an undetermined number of people—very different in opinion, social class, and personal style—who these days bear an anxiety so intense they hesitate to express it. They go about their business, but with an air of distraction, a fear that naming their fear may help bring it about. And they don't, of course, wish to seem parochial, or hysterical, or apocalyptic.

"I am one of these people and perhaps I can speak for them a little. We live with the thought that the men who hold power in the world are preparing a political course that will end with the destruction of Israel. Some do so out of malevolence, others out of no visible hostility—indeed, for the highest of motives—but all aim toward the same result. It would be good if we brought this fear into the open, good for us personally and as a way of stirring ourselves into action."[13]

It was also an "outsider," Hans Morgenthau, who offered the only professional critique of the Kissinger policy in the Middle East that any of the mass media noted for a long time (only because he had acquired a wide reputation as a critic of the Vietnam policy). The gist of Professor Hans Morgenthau's argument was that this policy renders Israel defenseless, save for worthless international guarantees and dubious Arab promises to spare her. "When Neville Chamberlain went to Munich, he had no intention of destroying Czechoslovakia; he thought instead that he had assured peace in our time. On his death-bed, the former Prime Minister remarked that everything would have turned out all right if Hitler had not lied to him. Let us hope," concluded Morgenthau, "Henry Kissinger will not have occasion to assert that everything in the Middle East would have turned out all right if Sadat had not lied to him."[14] When echoed on television, these words were the only doubts concerning Kissinger's Middle East policy that could at all reach the broader American public.

part two
Kissinger in American Eyes

3. The Media: Superman

When Americans expressed their admiration for Henry Kissinger, it was for reasons very different from those that stirred deep feelings about him among Arabs and Jews in the Middle East. A catalogue of qualities and achievements publicly ascribed to him would make some saints appear insignificant by comparison; his status in the age of mass media and public relations, was probably the equivalent of medieval sainthood. In the Middle East, he was said to have turned ancient antagonists toward the path of peace; to have transformed hostile millions of Arabs suddenly into warm friends of America; to have ejected the Russians from Egypt and other Arab states; and more. His skills were nothing short of miraculous: his diplomacy bridged conflicts too deep for other practitioners of the craft; he healed historical enmities; he had uncanny gifts for making bitter antagonists empathize. He was termed "miracle man" and "superman."

The leaders of the United States declared Henry Kissinger an enormous "national asset," "indispensable," whose removal from office would, in the opinion of President Ford, be "disastrous" for America and the world. His threat of resignation sent shivers through the majestic assembly of United States Senators and through the country. He was treated as an invaluable resource for which the whole world clamored. If the trag-

31

edy of Ireland seemed to run over, there were urgings that
America lend Kissinger to the troubled peoples over there for a
while; and that what the struggling Greeks and Turks on Cyprus
needed was Kissinger.

The tendency was to glimpse the miraculous in all his doings,
including ordinary things. Mass circulation journals divulged
"How Henry Does It." A *Time* cover (April 1, 1974) thus
portrayed Kissinger as magician, producing the peace dove from
his hat, before the awed leaders of the world. In trying to
dampen such adulation, serious journalism usually endorsed it,
though in a less vulgar form, discussing his miracles, but putting the word between quotation marks; or ascribing phenom-
enal accomplishments to him while reminding readers that even
he is only a mortal and ought not to be expected to do everything; as one columnist concluded, sometimes "even a Kissinger can't work his peace-making miracles."[1]

Historians will surely ponder the roots of this extraordinary personality cult; but some answers are already apparent,
and they point unsurprisingly first to the immense power and
remarkable vulnerability of the communications media in contemporary America. As a study of the subject by Roger Morris,
formerly a member of Kissinger's staff at the National Security
Council, shows, the media have told the American people about
this man pretty much what he wanted them to know. As a result, Americans know Kissinger's successes—both real and
imagined—while his failures, some of truly catastrophic proportions, are not readily apparent or indeed visible.

Wrote Morris: "Partly as a result of Kissinger's energetic
accessibility, the media, while covering Kissinger and what he
has concentrated upon, have a tendency to ignore what he
ignores. Not only do we thus lack an accounting of the weaknesses or oversights of a singularly powerful Secretary of State;
more important, there is the danger that public and Congressional attention will not fasten on issues—even urgent ones—
that are not to Kissinger's taste. Foreign economic policy is
probably the most significant case in point.

"The most recent example of neglect of an economic issue by both Kissinger and the media who cover him is the increasingly grave world food problem. It isn't seen as a 'Kissinger' story. Both the Government and the media have tended to treat the global food scarcities of 1973–1974 as an aberration, the product of the unusual Soviet purchases or temporary market fluctuations. Yet some experts warn with rising alarm that the problem is becoming chronic, due to the unchecked population growth, massive grain imports by the U.S.S.R., limits on yields of vegetable and fish protein, and the rapid dwindling of world grain reserves. It is Kissinger—the man who holds dramatic airport press conferences—who makes U.S. foreign policy on food. Yet he has received only the most perfunctory questioning on this topic."[2]

Morris mentioned that Fred Bergsten, Kissinger's assistant for international economic affairs from 1969 to 1971, has described his record on economics as "dismal." When Kissinger got involved in these affairs, "he usually bungled badly." Early in 1969, he impaired relations with Japan by seeking to force trade concessions in the return of Okinawa; relations with Europe were poisoned by similar insensitivity to economic issues; the enormous wheat sale to the Russians now haunts American consumers and hungry masses of other continents; his magic was not in evidence as the dollar and the international monetary system collapsed in 1971. American economic foreign policy, said Bergsten, had been damaged by Kissinger's idiosyncratic (Lone Ranger) diplomatic style and realpolitik visions from another age, as well as by maneuvering aimed at securing his personal power in the White House.

When Bergsten circulated this analysis late in 1973, it struck people in Washington as strangely new, since Kissinger's sorry record had been ignored by the media. His essay was rejected by *The Washington Post* and *The New Republic* before *The New York Times* agreed to print it on its Op-Ed page on December 12. Morris added that *The Times* had earlier not printed a sensational and solid story by its correspondent Tad

Szulc on the American-Vietnamese invasion of Cambodia upon the request of Kissinger. Another important report, by William Beecher, *The Times* Pentagon correspondent, on the December 1972 bombing of North Vietnam, contradicting the Kissinger version of events, was belatedly printed in a "cut down" version. The discomfort with which serious and otherwise courageous journals regard material critical of Kissinger was more recently illustrated by the refusal of the *Saturday Review/World* to publish a story it had commissioned Tad Szulc to write, a profile of the Secretary. Morris explained that what the journal had wanted, according to its editor, Norman Cousins, was "what was behind the Kissinger miracles, his ability to win confidence from people on many sides," and instead Szulc raised some sober doubts about the man, which, though "entirely valid and raised by a competent man," were not deemed fit for publication.

This extraordinary immunity from criticism granted by the media to Kissinger was manifested also in the curious manner in which an aggressively investigative press, in pursuit of all possible implications of the greatest scandal in American political history, managed for so long not even a glance in the direction of one of the most intimate participants in Richard Nixon's administration. Just as the affair was about to vanish, there appeared barely a hint of inquisitiveness that Kissinger quickly nipped in the bud in a manner as imperious as it was incredible. He angrily told the press to cease questioning him forthwith and accept instead the answer of a Senate committee to his threat of resignation—which was never in doubt. Tom Wicker analyzed the maneuver as follows.

"Henry Kissinger happens to be about the shrewdest manipulator of the press ever to get himself quoted as a 'senior official' telling the public what he wants it to know. The major effect of his Salzburg performance was to get the United States Senate virtually on record that he was an honest man who ought not to be questioned by the bloodthirsty press. Mr. Kissinger also created considerable public sympathy for himself and shifted the focus of the controversy; now the question is not so much whether he did anything he shouldn't have, but whether the press should have raised such embarrassing questions about a man who was busily creating a generation of peace."[3]

The evidence that had surfaced in the belated and less than half-hearted journalistic curiosity about Kissinger's role in Watergate was seriously incriminating and the Secretary's few attempts at coping with it much less than convincing. *The Times* was moved to take note of this, however apologetically, in an editorial shortly before the Salzburg ultimatum: "We regretfully observe that Secretary Kissinger seems to be vulnerable to the charge of dissembling about his role in this distasteful affair."[4] This role, according to some informants, transcended the mere "initiation" of taps, into the origins of the scandal as a whole. The Senators avoided any possibly incriminating evidence— "He is needed," explained Senator Humphrey, "He's a tremendous national asset"[5]—and voted unanimously to clear him. (The committee's chairman, Senator Fulbright, actually portrayed Kissinger as victim of a conspiracy by warmongering circles.) The press stopped asking questions.

But the press had already tended to exculpate Kissinger on such failings as had transpired before. As Roger Morris discovered, journalists like to look elsewhere for them: "Mistakes are caused by the vast anonymous beast called 'bureaucracy. They are temporary, unimportant, probably not worth a story. Not surprisingly, Kissinger privately encourages this view by complaining about bureaucratic undercutting or being 'spread too thin' Most commonly. he privately portrays himself—and is depicted by the press in turn—as holding the line against a martial foreign policy made in the Pentagon." (We have just encountered this in Fulbright's version of Kissinger's role in Watergate and will again meet it in the latter's version of the critical delay in aid to Israel in the October War.) The press accepts the notion of bureaucratic undercutting without investigation and ignores evidence that belies the anti-martial posture. Insinuating to the press, already hostile to the other people in the White House, that the blame somehow rests there, is another device, which David Halberstam termed "the Henry agony thing"—Kissinger assumes a very pained and helpless pose and reminds the journalists of the sort of people he is stuck with.[6]

And when failings cannot be laid to others, the tendency is to apologize for Kissinger. When Jack Anderson divulged the secret White House minutes in 1971, they revealed that Kissinger had lied to the press concerning the American anti-India stance in the war with Pakistan; he had termed reports to this effect "totally inaccurate." The respected Washington journalists Joseph Kraft and John Osborne, reacted to the disclosure by dwelling on the *motive* for the leak, censuring that rather than the lying.

It would be odd if such incredible performance by a nominally free press were genuinely spontaneous, and of course it is not. By all accounts, Kissinger came to the government with a deliberate policy to obtain as much as possible personal control of what the media would know, understand and communicate about him and his work. A basic rule—that only he could talk to journalists—was emphatically put to his staff at their first meeting, in January of 1969. He set about cultivating the press with an intensity extraordinary even by Washington standards. According to former co-workers in Washington, Kissinger must have spent close to half his time either dealing with the press or worrying about how to deal with them. Editors were amazed by their reporters' access and were often fascinated to get a call themselves from Kissinger with some apparent privileged information offered with a suggestion of intimacy. Reporter response to assiduous cultivation with ingratiation, flattery, disarming candor and charming dissimulation, and the sharing of rare information was no different from results with legislators, given the same treatment after Kissinger's accession to the State Department: "fawning gratitude," as one Congressman put it.[7] Kissinger "seduced" the press, which was exceedingly willing, said Fred Emory, *The Times* of London man in Washington; he had "the press eating out of his hand," added Harrison Salisbury.[8]

Kissinger generated for himself public relations power, quite independent of his office, as a folk hero in the world of the sensational press, movie magazines and gossip columnists; in short, acquiring "star quality." That world seized on the drab professor in a frantic pace of Hollywood parties, dates with movie stars in glittering places, and fascinating rumors. Once in motion, promotional processes feed on themselves: having become a star by association with others in the folk culture, one can leave it to the promoters of new hopefuls to advertise their association with the star, thus further enhancing his stardom. The translation of social power into political power—for instance, in public recognition and approval—is a phenomenon that has already widely been noted in the case of the Kennedy brothers. It doubtless accounts for much of the power of Kissinger, who carried the style into the political arena as well. The effect is to have even the serious press focus on personality rather than policy, on method rather than substance. "It's more like covering Marilyn Monroe," Morris quotes Stanley Karnow, "than a secretary of state." In Washington, Kissinger is regarded as his own best public relations man.

The more compelling the need to cover Kissinger, the greater his power over reporters. If a reporter were to lose access to Kissinger, either because he was tough or critical, his editors would seek another who could cover Kissinger rather than back their own man. Self-censorship accounts for failures fully to cover the man and his policies at least as much as any conscious effort on his part to orchestrate the news. The power increases with access and intimacy, peaking in fact in those escapades of peripatetic diplomacy—as in the Middle East— which the public has received as his greatest successes. The pressures on journalists are greatly intensified when traveling with Kissinger. In his Washington press conferences, Kissinger is ingratiating and intimate and maintains a "clubby" atmosphere with flattery and humor.

A rare exposition of these press conferences in the press was rendered by Martin Arnold: "To the 20 or so reporters who regularly cover the State Department, he is virtually the only source in town, so a Kissinger news conference, like the one he held Friday, is a pretty clubby happening. In the end, the reporters don't exactly report hard news so much as give their readers, viewers and listeners an exegesis of the range of philosophical pronouncements delivered by the Secretary of State." He described the ritual as starting with a game of "liar's poker," played not with cards but with serial numbers on dollar bills, in anticipation of Kissinger's arrival. The esoteric game separates the regulars who accompany him abroad from the fifty or sixty other reporters who might cover a conference. The Secretary starts each conference with a joke, aimed at relaxing the reporters as well as showing them that he really understands their business. The regulars congregate in the front-row seats and the Secretary shows intimacy with them by calling them by their first names, "Murrey," "Barry," or "Marv." According to John Herbers, White House correspondent for *The Times*, "All the bloated bags in Washington, the bureau chiefs, the State Department reporters, the White House correspondents—the most self-important group in Washington—attend these things."[9]

At least twenty reporters asked questions in the above conference, but the only information they got was an item the Secretary wanted them to have, something many felt could have been obtained in a two-minute telephone call to the State Department. "Mr. Kissinger meets with his top aides before the conference to decide what he wants to come out of the news conference and only very occasionally will the scenario be upset." Not only are unwelcome questions answered in a very general way, but supplementaries required to develop information are also not really possible. According to Arnold, many newsmen are unhappy over their editors' news judgment and wish they did not automatically put a Kissinger news conference story on page one; many also feel that there could be more investigative reporting of the State Department, there being other ways to get a diplomatic story than by speaking personally to Mr. Kissinger.

" 'Kissinger lies to all of us,' said another State Department correspondent [to a fellow journalist from *The New York Post*] . . . . Few journalists seem indignant at the Secretary of State's alleged lying; most tend to regard it as a sort of diplomatic necessity. They also realize that they have little choice but to 'accept what he says'—since Kissinger is their source, their only source in the arena he has constructed of one-man shuttle diplomacy. Some even grudgingly admire his proficiency at prevarication. . . ."[10]

Travel with Kissinger turns into an incessant press conference in almost total insulation from the rest of the world. He tells reporters jokes, briefs them incessantly and regularly supplies them with his own interpretation of the news he made in each capital. He threatens to punish them—in a joking sort of way—if they were to write anything unfavorable about him. But the usual pressures and his own management suffice to prevent this from happening. There is usually neither time nor energy left to evaluate events critically. Role-confusion among his journalistic travel companions is rife. "Have you got anything coming up that'll embarrass us?" Morris cited one investigative reporter recalling being asked by a worried diplomatic reporter who was about to depart on a Kissinger trip. "It was the *'us'* that really killed me," the reporter added.

Identification with the person they are supposed to observe with detachment is furthered by the tendency of journalists in foreign capitals and at home to "scoop" accompanying reporters as if they were members of his staff (and he supplies them bits of rare information, which furthers the illusion). Working in a world of glamour and glitter, the diplomatic press corps views itself as more special, more privy to great affairs of state than other journalists; but they do less investigative reporting and are more dependent on government than the others. Since they usually bring no independent intellectual framework to data they obtain, their interpretation of news is conformist and conventional. The author of an elaborate profile of Kissinger's thought found that the hundreds of journalistic stories about the man show little familiarity with it, even though his writings are readily available.[11]

There was also the special circumstance of Watergate and other scandals that added to Kissinger's importance to the press. Engaged in a gigantic struggle with the government at the very top, the press, with *The Washington Post* in the lead, was loath to sever itself completely from high-ranking officials. Being one of the few high officials in Washington who would talk to journalists, Kissinger was important to them. In this war the press had to protect its flank and so made a separate peace with Kissinger: he would talk to them and they would not probe him.

But the dynamic factor, by all accounts, is "the well-known ego of Henry Kissinger," as Henry Brandon once put it,[12] in one variation of a common theme. Men who have been intimately associated with him speak of a personality structure that craves massive approval bordering on pathology.

"To some who saw Kissinger at close range within the government," recalled Morris, "his easy mastery of the media held a paradox. The poised, charming statesman at the microphone was also the insecure, shy, anxious man back in the office who worried about trivialities, often painfully ill at ease in personal encounters. His favorite comment about anti-war demonstrators was, 'They don't know who they are.' Yet, that diagnosis might have applied to the man himself. Despite his awesome success, he seemed self-consciously the German Jewish immigrant, ever an outsider in the American foreign policy establishment. Thus his deliberate aversion to Middle East diplomacy until, as a close friend remembers him confiding last summer, 'I am secretary of state and more my own man.'

"That lack of self-confidence and identity may well explain too his reluctance to become involved in human rights issues, or to appear 'soft' in those he did deal with. If the Averell Harrimans could risk compassion without fearing that their motives or objectivity would be questioned, it was not the same for Kissinger, or so he apparently felt. Similarly, the man so clearly in command of the substance of issues seemed to need as well the support of personal fealty. 'Remember,' he once whispered to me after an uncomfortable meeting at which some of us had dissented on the planned invasion of Cambodia, 'I supported *you* on African policy.' It was an arguable point, but the same insecurity and urge to personalize explain Kissinger's ardent attention to press relations *and* his acute sensitivity to criticism. 'No secretary of state has paid more attention to the media,' I said to one official. 'No secretary of state has felt so much he needed to,' he shot back."

A term recurring in interviews with Kissinger's earlier acquaintances is "paranoia." A man who knew him at Harvard recalled: "Henry used to joke a lot about his paranoia but in fact he was somewhat ruled by it. For prolonged periods of time he was not on speaking terms with many people. He had this fear of his competitors, this extraordinary need to be liked and appreciated, this fear that behind his back people were laughing. I feel certain that if a proper mental diagnosis had been made in 1962 he would have been declared sick."[13]

Anthony Lake, another former member of Kissinger's staff has written that the man himself "has helped create a situation in which he must be taken on an all or nothing basis."[14] Other associates have privately rendered a sketch of the man, from which it appears that his idea of discussion is an authoritative exposition by himself while others applaud. (A Kissinger aide, announcing forthcoming sessions with the new President Ford, slipped in using the word "educational" when referring to them, quickly adding that he would like the word deleted in print.)[15] "For the truth is," writes Tad Szulc, "that Henry Kissinger, the owner of one of America's most monumental egos, can function effectively only as a superman and superstar in his own right. . . . Kissinger has such a thirst for applause and adulation that he can brook no questioning or criticism in any area of his activities.[16]

And on a related trait, Richard Holbrooke has written, "it is significant to note that that many of the people who distrust him most are those who know him best. Almost everyone who knows him well, even his strongest supporters, says that he cannot be trusted."[17]

The pursuit of either/or is intense, petulant and petty. A French publisher of a book offensive to the Secretary thus finds himself expelled from this country (a State Department spokesman denying that the Department had taken any action against the alien, an Immigration and Naturalization Service official confirming it).[18] The illicit prying into the lives of closest associates is generally known; less so are attempts at enlisting cooperation of foreign potentates for silencing opponents at home, thus American Jews via Israeli leaders. The appearance of rare dissent from the universal applause for Kissinger's Middle East ventures immediately triggered pressures to desist and an attempt to silence a leading dissenter, Hans Morganthau, by coopting him to the Secretary's entourage, as a "special" adviser. Even as the domestic scene is remarkable for the scarcity of the usual checks and scrutiny of his work, he reportedly complains to foreign statesmen of vast and vicious forces poised against him at home.[19] In response to questioning by the press on discrepancies between his statements on his role in Watergate, he produced a national crisis, threatening resignation if the questioning was not silenced.

Ronald Steel wrote that Kissinger's traits emerge even from the Kalbs' "laundered account" (Kissinger) very clearly: "One sees his hypersensitivity to criticism, his insistence on personalizing any disagreement, his self-pity and much advertised paranoia, his lack of self-confidence (which may explain his fear of appearing 'soft' and his hard-line position of military policy), his insensitivity to those serving under him, and his obsequiousness toward those of higher standing."[20]

Kissinger's use of secret government surveillance for control of the press was more characteristic of totalitarian regimes than any democratic system, particularly as it involved Marvin Kalb, Henry Brandon and Joseph Kraft, men already widely known for their loyalty to him. "What are we to make of that?" wondered Daniel Ellsberg, a man who both knows Kissinger personally and quite a lot about such practices. "Part of his thinking was given by a White House aide who said Kissinger wanted to see whether, behind his back, these journalists and his own White House assistants were loyal to him. And he wanted to find out if these people had other sources that were contradicting what he was saying.

"Nobody has made this inference: Imagine the ability Kissinger acquired to manipulate those individuals with whom he was working and talking to daily or weekly, when he secretly knew all they were saying to their other sources and associates. In other words, Kissinger knew by these wiretaps logs whether he was getting through to those guys, what to emphasize, how to change his pitch, how to counter a position credibly, and very persuasively, in a way the newsmen could never recognize was based on secret knowledge. And it was precisely those people who were most friendly to him that he had a great desire to be able to control.

"In fact, the leaks from the FBI indicated that he had asked directly for those taps and that *they* had insisted on presidential authority for such taps. That was when he turned to the President and got *him* involved."[21]

4. Personal Success or National Interest

The fact that Henry Kissinger has achieved enormous personal success cannot be argued; what remains to be established in large measure is the success of his foreign policy. It is indeed a measure of the first kind of success that the two are almost always being confused and mistaken for each other. The conditions render public discussion, scrutiny and evaluation of policy enormously difficult, if not impossible. The subservience of the press impairs the lifeline of debate; how judge anything when denied reasonably reliable information? In these circumstances, the press conveys a selective portrayal of events which may obscure most relevant ones; and those cited are dubious. While showing little zeal in fulfilling its investigative function, the press discourages others from filling the slack, offering them little hospitality in its pages when they do appear and reducing the likelihood of their appearance in the first place, by sustaining a sterile and conformist climate of opinion. The obvious dangers to the political system from such failure of the fourth estate need not be belabored here.

Other political institutions have not checked the press in this failure, as the press checked Watergate. Rather, most of Washington became a cheering section for the media hero, as Leslie Gelb concluded.[1] The Congress was awed by the miraculous achievements ascribed to Kissinger. "As a Senate staff

member put it, 'There's nothing like success for gaining support
up here.' " Like the media, the Congress has largely substituted
ovation, even evasion of unpleasant evidence, for critical investigative function. Indeed elected officials appear even more
reluctant than journalists to question a folk hero. If anything, the
deepened insecurities in Watergate and the presidential transi-
tion strengthened the notion of Kissinger's indispensability, because of a natural tendency to stick to the true and tested in
such trials. The incoming President was eager to reassure the
country that, come what may, it can count on Kissinger's staying on in his administration. Russell Baker has suggested that
Kissinger has made himself indispensable in that, having run
foreign policy alone and peripatetically, only he knows what
the policy is. "Everybody knows it is brilliant, but nobody, including the President, knows why."[2]

Kissinger's tendency to treat debate of policy as pernicious
warfare, and his insistence on being taken on an all or nothing
basis, further distorted what little there was of it. A former
member of his staff, Anthony Lake, warned that, "the greater
the hero worship, the shriller the critics sound and become."
Frustrated by the uncritical acclaim for him from so many
quarters, those who still speak out can easily fall into the trap
of at least appearing to make unfair, sweeping, *ad hominem*
assaults on his character and even competence. Up against hero
worship, legitimate criticism begins to sound like ungrateful
grousing.[3] And should the tide ever run against him, censure
could be as unfairly sweeping as approval. In connection with
Kissinger's imperious attitude toward dissent it seems worth-
while to mention the view of many observers that the man appears more comfortable in dealing with authoritarian and totalitarian foreign leaders than with democratic ones.

It is, of course, not as if there is no public criticism of Kissinger and his policy—we have just reviewed some of it here;
but it is sporadic and has, with perhaps just one exception,
détente, failed to engage American opinion in a real debate. His
adulation by politicians and the media obscures serious mis-
givings in many quarters about his nature and his policies. "The

problem," Ronald Steel has written, "is not Mr. Kissinger's abilities, but the message he has used and the values that underlie him. Like the President he so lately served, Mr. Kissinger is indifferent to ideology, obsessed with secrecy, and mesmerized by the game of power politics."[4]

Both the means and the ends of his policy have alarmed experts close to the foreign affairs establishment. "But if he has become a hero to Americans," wrote Richard Holbrooke, "let us hope that he does not become a model. His style and spirit run counter to some of this nation's deep and enduring values. Perhaps in the aftermath of Vietnam we needed a diplomat who turned away from the excessive moralism of a John Foster Dulles or a Dean Rusk. In showing what could be done when released from certain moral and political blinders, Kissinger did us all a great service.

"But he carries amoralism too far. In public statements, he hedges his bets, tries to straddle both sides of the fence, as he did in his speech to *Pacem in Terris III* in October 1973: 'America cannot be true to itself without moral purpose. This country has always had a sense of mission. . . .' But in context, the sentences . . . seem like throwaway lines. The message is clearly in what follows: America must free itself from its myths.

"But one man's myths may be another's guiding purpose. The dividing line cannot be defined; too much of one extreme is not a cure for the other extreme. If Kissinger had been Secretary of State for a different sort of President, things might have been very different. But, in this sense, the gymnasium professor's son from Furth and the scrub football player from Whittier were a perfect match; Nixon's style and values also seem alien to certain central American traditions. Only in Nixon's case, in his disregard for those values, he crossed the last lines of restraint, and moved into active participation in impeachable offenses. It is interesting that while Kissinger was subtly emphasizing the differences between himself and the other members of Mr. Nixon's entourage, in fact there are some real similarities. How uncomfortable did Kissinger really feel about the covert behavior of Haldeman and Ehrlichman, provided that it wasn't directed at him? How 'distasteful' did

Kissinger really find those activities he now deplores but clearly was party to, such as the wiretapping of his own staff?"[5]

The present, wrote Thomas Hughes, is a time sorely in need of many imaginative men and coherent public understanding and participation in foreign policy. Instead, our nation has made "an exceptional overinvestment in one exceptional man—Henry Kissinger—who has made some exceptional gains of uncertain durability. In the process, our national priorities have perforce become his preferences. Our national interests have become whatever he has time for at the moment."

He warned of grave jeopardy to the national interest in the very essence of Kissingerian policy—personalism, marked by personal deals, secrecy, abhorrence of institutional restraints, and emasculation of debate. Personal relationships with foreign leaders can encourage misunderstandings as easily as understandings and produce false as well as realistic expectations. Fraught with the consequent dangers of disappointment, and sudden reversibility, personalism also cannot well cement real gains, leaving little room for institutionalized loyalties in both the government and the country.

"Personalism, therefore, often tends to prefer the superficial and the transitory over the deep and fundamental. Personalism has a short-term timetable. It is tempted to take benefits now and leave the unknown costs to its successors. The more intractable the problem and far-reaching the measures required to meet it, the more a narrow leadership will be tempted to indulge in pseudo-solutions for appearances' sake. Personalism tends to deal with the thin crust of affairs, to concentrate on personal arrangements for the moment rather than partnership arrangements for the future.

"Personalism gives priority to other personalism often gravitating to personal counterparts who can always be found on the authoritarian side of the East-West agenda. It tends to filter out the larger galaxy of the public issues of North-South and West-West relations. Thus our policy toward genocide, militarism, and self-determination in the vast Indian subcontinent becomes a simple function to a decrepit Pakistani government's willingness to facilitate our first secret trip to Peking.

Thus personalism pulls us into personal embraces with authoritarian personalities in Madrid and Lisbon while praising their 'moral courage' literally hours or days before they are assassinated, expelled, or overthrown. Every sheikh in the Persian Gulf insists on nothing less than the Secretary's personal attention.

"Consequently, personalism has to become fastidiously restrictive in determining how a small entourage spends its time in a narrowly chosen field. Personalism breeds selectivity of an often idiosyncratic kind. The greater the selectivity, the greater the other issues which are ignored, short-circuited, suppressed, or bypassed. However vital the issues chosen for the great man's concentrated attention, his whims are determining, and a host of other issues pile up on his desk or enter the dustbin of history. Usually these will be the vital longer-term global issues that require many men and measures—the complex economic, cultural, social, institutional issues which do not lend themselves easily to the high drama of high-wire acts."[6]

Meanwhile, said Hughes, dashes of miracle and mystery obscure from us what really happens in our foreign relations. "As the euphoria diminishes, the onlookers will begin to distinguish between our foreign policy as it has recently been perceived and our foreign policy as it has actually been pursued. The omissions, costs, and contradictions will come to the fore." One likely cost is deeper public cynicism and reversion to isolationism and sullenness in governmental bureaucracy.

Some apprehensions had been bolstered by the first serious probe by Tad Szulc into Kissinger's handling of the Vietnam ceasefire negotiations. The analysis, based on heretofore unpublished documents, revealed deception, manipulation and resort to brutal violence, which to England's *The Sunday Times* (June 2, 1974), spelled no less than "The Mind of a Modern Machiavelli" for a heading.

Such revelations had little impact on American opinion for much the same reason that little attention was paid to the obvious sham of the "cease-fire" that was achieved only on paper. So long as Kissinger got results—extricating America from the South-East Asia morass—people were more than willing to ignore his deviousness; it added in effect a tinge of endearing naughtiness to their hero. In the language of the contemporary scandals, America was seen to have in him an amazing "super-plumber," except that this one really used skulduggery in the national interest. (This view probably played a part in popular acquiescence in the Senate's reluctance to probe Kissinger's role in Watergate.) But neither have other revelations, touching on the approved results and the "sure hand" of the man, had more impact. Szulc's analysis indicates that the vaunted realism—Kissinger's strong card in defense of amoral policy—failed to grasp the Vietnamese reality for some three years.[7] Also, he got the agreement pretty much on North Vietnamese terms and might well have had it before the United States launched the awesome bombing campaign in the North in December of 1972. The death and destruction there, wrote Szulc, was wielded not to bring about a change in Hanoi's stance so much as to demonstrate to Saigon our readiness to "brutalize" its foe, to induce it to sign an agreement all but reached with Hanoi. And America is, of course, still deeply involved in Vietnam, after all that.

The only critique of Kissinger policies that engaged American opinion in earnest concerns détente with the Soviet Union. There arose considerable resistance to granting Moscow trade concessions without reciprocity in the matter of human rights, specifically in the emigration of Soviet Jews and the treatment of dissenting intellectuals. The first mobilized American Jewry into a dynamic movement of protest and generated massive support in the Congress for the Jackson Amendment to the Trade Reform Act of 1973, denying credits and most-favored-nation status to any nation with a restrictive emigration policy; the latter cause stirred popular sympathies, even in liberal and leftist quarters, particularly for the famed dissenters, Solzhenitsyn and Sakharov. Kissinger's claim that human rights must be separated from détente with the Russians seemed not to have been acceptable to the people and their representatives in Washington.

The other facet of détente involving a major political struggle concerned the Kissinger approach to arms limitations agreements with the Soviet Union. Here a serious dispute be-

tween the Department of State and the Pentagon was acknowledged by President Ford. Allied with Defense against the Secretary of State were Congressmen grouped around Senator
Henry Jackson and various other groups, including leading students of Soviet and international affairs. To the Senate Foreign
Relations Committee and foreign diplomats, Kissinger portrayed
his opposition as a "military-industrial-intellectual complex"
committed to the continuation of cold-war policies of confrontation with Moscow, jeopardizing survival itself in the
nuclear age.

Critics of Kissinger argued that the issue was distorted,
saying it was not whether to strive for détente with the Soviet
Union but whether he achieved genuine détente. A critical mani-
festo in the Spring, 1974, issue of *International Relations*, was
prepared by some of them, a galaxy of those studying the
Soviet Union and international affairs, including Bernard Lewis,
Robert Conquest, Richard Pipes, and Leonard Schapiro, among
others. They held that the Soviet Union used détente in the
hope of achieving, not peaceful accommodation, but a decisive
shift of the world balance of power in its favor. They called attention to the pattern of unilateral American concessions running through the web of arms, economic and political agreements constituting the Kissinger policy of détente. They pointed
out that this policy reduced neither global competition between
the super-powers and ideological enmity in Soviet writings nor
the burdensome armament race. They held that human rights in
the Soviet Union—far from being irrelevant—were in effect a
touchstone of genuine détente, as opposed to a manipulative
posture. These arguments appeared to strike sympathetic chords
in wide segments of opinion, particularly in the aftermath of the
October War in the Middle East, in which the Russians' role
caused disappointment and even bitterness almost generally in
the United States. There was widespread anxiety that foolish
and dangerous actions might be taken in defense of Kissinger's
stake in his détente policy. His public praise of Soviet "restraint" in that war was almost everywhere greeted with disbelief. Kissinger's admission of weakness on détente was mani-

fested in the summer of 1974 in spurring creation of a national committee of notables in defense of the policy, and, unusual for him, calling for a national debate on détente; then an apparent readiness to bargain in earnest with the Jackson forces on Jewish emigration, after persistently seeking their surrender, by various means, including warnings that the "Jewish issue" endangered global peace. Having obtained economic concessions from the Congress for the Russians in return for his claim to have their assurance for a relaxation of restrictions on the emigration of Jews and dissidents, it suddenly appeared that the deal might be fraudulent. Not only did the Russians produce a letter to Kissinger emphatically repudiating any such understanding before passage of the trade bill, but they also unleashed a propaganda barrage at home which intimidated potential emigrants. An impression obtained quickly that the Russians had through Kissinger obtained what they wanted from America for nothing.[8] They risked no economic gains and even helped discredit the Jackson forces when they cancelled their 1972 trade agreement with the United States.

Kissinger joined the debate in characteristic fashion: going to the Vladivostok summit in December, 1974, and claiming triumphal "breakthrough" in arms limitation with the Soviet Union and "capping" the armament race, due to the fact that the latter had made "very major concessions." As always, he warned his critics of global disaster if the deal fell through. As soon as the agreement was publicized, there was almost general dismay, as even his backers on détente complained, that, while they preferred the agreement to nothing at all, he had exaggerated it. "Mr. Kissinger's style," wrote Anthony Lewis, "is catching up with him. The oversell, the personal dramas, the Hairbreadth Harry escapes, the insistence that disaster will strike if he is not allowed to play the game by his own secret rules—it is all becoming too familiar to too many people."[9]

An earlier threat to Kissinger's standing developed in the summer of 1974, as revelations about his involvement in the overthrow of the Allende regime in Chile a year earlier coincided with public unhappiness over the course of the war in

Cyprus. The Chile affair showed Kissinger, once again, to have deceived the Senate Foreign Relations Committee and revealed him as a Cold War warrior, just as he was accusing critics of his détente policy as being just that.[10] The Secretary did not address the issues and was relieved by a public endorsement and exoneration by President Ford. While the matter impaired Kissinger's "liberal" image, it failed to stir any real public debate of his policies or modes of operation. The Cyprus affair had a greater public and political impact, in part because of the mobilization of large numbers of Greek-Americans and because the usual defense of realpolitik appeared to be failing. If Kissinger's posture was in this war again amoral, it seemed dubious on purely pragmatic grounds as well. *The New York Times* accused him editorially, on September 14, of having "bungled American policy in the Cyprus crisis" and the Congress was moved to inhibit aid to Turkey, despite strong resistance by Ford. Though Cyprus tarnished Kissinger's reputation for having a sure hand, it triggered no comprehensive debate either. The Secretary's rejoinder to the setbacks was more public relations activity and breathtaking travel. An extensively cited interview with James Reston, who has served before as sympathetic Kissinger interpreter, presented him once again as philosopher-statesman consummately concerned over the highest aspirations of the nation and the world (announcing, incidentally, that the Middle East conflict was already half-solved, after just a year on the job).[11] Soon after, the media were replete with excitement from nearly a dozen-and-a-half countries around the world, as the Secretary was seen preventing war in the Middle East, healing rifts over Cyprus, soothing the Russians, lowering the price of oil, lubricating a new agreement with Spain, feeding India and Bangladesh, reassuring Pakistan, etc. His particular attraction toward involvement in Middle Eastern affairs was apparent in the time and energy he devoted to them on the tour. As the notorious global tinderbox, the region would seem to justify all that attention by the American Secretary; but also it was not improbable that, in a time of waning popularity, he was attracted to a region especially well endowed with the elements that give rise to acclaim at home.

Indeed, the one area of Kissinger policy on which virtually no criticism was heard is the Middle East. What public discussion of his Middle East policy existed was, with rare exceptions, pretty close to ovation. Considering the importance usually attributed in the United States to that part of the world and the great anxieties its reputation for volatility engendered, the virtual absence of any scrutiny or debate of a policy for the area and the almost total reliance on Kissinger was truly extraordinary. Indeed, the few critics of Kissinger's other policies usually insisted on reassuring us there was no need of scrutiny of his Middle East policy. Their tenor was that unlike the Middle East, where he performed brilliant feats, he was open to criticism in other areas of policy, say, economic or European. His critics appeared to use the Middle East policy both as a balancer of criticism (proving their fairness by giving the man his due, where appropriate) and as a standard of excellence against which to evaluate his other policies. Thus one critic of his Cyprus policy, Graham Hovey, thought it lacked, in dealing with allies, the "sensitivity" that was an ingredient of his success in the Middle East.[12]

A rare exception was Tad Szulc, who, while essentially in agreement with the general judgment, raised some questions concerning the *modus operandi* of the Secretary and even the adequacy of his concept of Middle Eastern reality, suggesting that it may be "over-intellectualized." While sharing the popular belief in a new movement toward peace in the area, Szulc doubted that the weakening of Israel in this process was in the national interest of the United States, and held that Kissinger's opening to the Arabs was greatly overrated. "The 'friendship' with the Arabs," he wrote, "evolved almost entirely on Arab terms, which is not exactly a diplomatic miracle. A situation was created which set a precedent for future Arab blackmail. The immensely important question of why the United States has allowed itself to become so vulnerable is a separate matter, although it should be noted that as the head of the National Security Council, Kissinger failed to concern himself with oil five years ago."[13]

The question was not that serious doubts concerning Kissinger's Middle East policy had not been raised, but why they failed to stir public interest. Afterall, graver doubts than these were voiced earlier by Hans Morgenthau, and even he, widely regarded as the first true prophet in the Vietnamese tragedy, could not arouse much questioning of the policy. The general public was probably unaware of these doubts, since they were aired almost exclusively in limited circles; the sophisticated elite were not entirely unaware of them yet displayed no marked concern or curiosity, probably because many shared the premises of the policy and were prepared to acquiesce even in its less ideal aspects. Few in Washington believed the Kissinger version of his role in the October War and fewer still deemed it worthy of public challenge. When Leslie Gelb first mentioned in print this casual knowledge of what in fact amounted to a betrayal of a friendly nation in a time of trial, it hardly caused a ripple among those outside the Capital concerned with foreign policy.[14] Neither did Szulc's more elaborate exposition later.[15]

Kissinger's relative immunity from serious questioning by the press and the politicians thus appeared in the area of Middle East policy to be extended also to an international affairs elite that had not forsaken disbelief in other areas of policy. The likelihood of public scrutiny of United States policy in a region deemed vital in this manner shrank to next to nothing. The danger in such a condition would have been apparent even if no particular questions troubled complacence. But troubling questions abound, beyond those already cited.

Orientalists have long agreed that the roots of Arab antagonism to the Jewish state are deep and intractable. Why did this change radically, as the Secretary claimed? The media in the United States endorsed this claim, but what was the evidence in the Arab world itself? The Secretary claimed unprecedented movement toward peaceful settlement in the Middle East under his aegis. Was anything novel in this lingering conflict? Arabs and Israelis had already met in Geneva under international auspices before—indeed, over twenty years ago—to resolve their differences and even seemed at one time much closer to agreement than in 1974. What was unprecedented about military talks between Arabs and Israelis under United Nations chairmanship, as in the acclaimed Egyptian-Israeli talks at Kilometer 101? This was in fact commonplace along all of Israel's borders with Arab military and civilian officers for over two decades—during which period they managed to fight several wars and advance not at all toward peace.

The Arabs were said to agree—thanks to Kissinger's diplomacy—to direct negotiations with Israel for the first time. The main negotiations on disengagement so far were indirect; informal, direct contacts took place over the past fifty years, just as sporadically; the Kissinger forum in Geneva was acceptable to the Arabs, because it required of them nothing new, nothing they had not always conceded, by consenting to sit with Israeli delegates and others in meeting halls at the United Nations. The Kissinger policy presumed that Arab acceptance of the Jewish state was more likely within the narrow, virtually indefensible borders before the June War of 1967 than after. Yet no such development took place during the nearly two decades that these borders were the reality.

The Kissinger policy put high priority on securing Israeli withdrawal from Sinai and other territories—a formula that had failed to heal the conflict more than once in the past. The United States actually forced Israel to withdraw from Sinai after her first war with the Arabs, in 1948; then again, after her second war, in 1956; having obtained Israeli withdrawal from land lost by the Arabs in their fourth war, in 1973, it pressed in 1974 for withdrawal from more land, lost by the Arabs in the third war, in 1967. Why should the Arabs ever face up to the Jewish state, if the United States in effect insured their losses in every unsuccessful war with it?

The Kissinger policy claimed major success in displacing Soviet influence in Egypt and sought the same in other Arab nations. In view of the fact that America and Russia have displaced each other repeatedly in the past there, what could the real worth of such an achievement be? How weighty was American influence with Egypt in the aftermath of the last Israeli withdrawal from Sinai that the United States had achieved—or later, during the many years in which the United States helped feed her teeming masses, while she made war in Yemen (with American political support)? Did Americans not believe that the Russians had been thrown out of Egypt before, in 1972, only to discover that they were very much involved in Egypt's attack on Israel just one year later?

Why should we trust Egypt now, in view of this dismal record? The answers from Washington were that we had a new, different Egypt to deal with. Sadat is not Nasser—not consumed with hostility for Israel but with passion for Egypt's domestic progress—exactly what was said about Nasser when the United States began courting *him*. More basically, why should the United States compete at all with the Russians for Arab favor—especially in promising to "deliver" Israel? The Kissinger message to the Arabs now resounded in their various capitals: work with us, for only we are capable of forcing Israel to satisfy your desires. This, too, is not new, only more shrill; Arab (and Soviet)[16] strategy was actually predicated on the virtual certainty of its being repeated. Yet for obvious political and moral considerations there were restraints on the United States that did not apply to the Russians, who could always outbid the United States with anti-Israeli promises. Competing with them for Arab favor at Israel's expense was like playing with dice loaded against the United States—there were short-term gains, but America must on this score lose in the end.

These questions raised a strong presumption that Kissinger's personal success was widely mistaken for successful national policy in the Middle East. Much of what was supposed to be novel and unprecedented in his approach to the Middle East appeared remarkably like old and compromised ploys and nostrums. The prima facie evidence suggested not so much a stern reappraisal of failed principles of policy as a more clever application of them. In view of Kissinger's reputation as conceptualizer and theoretician this would seem surprising; but the same suspicion loomed ever larger in the minds of students of foreign policy in other areas, who were astonished to see him emerge from their probing of events as mere negotiator rather than innovator. Even the Kalbs' admiring account (*Kissinger*), demotes him from architect of policy—on the grand opening to China and the accords with Russia—to its implementer, terming the Middle East, on which it accepts his version of events, a notable exception.

part three
Managing War

5. Sadat Waits

President Sadat was not alone in eager anticipation that it would take Henry Kissinger's particular talents to break the deadlock in the diplomatic search for a settlement to the June War in 1967. On just how it, or rather who, was to be broken, Sadat was specific, leaving little to the imagination. It was not enough, he told President Nixon, to press Israel, as Secretary Rogers was doing; she had to be "squeezed" into submission.[1]

Many in the Washington foreign policy community must have had similar thoughts. Pondering Kissinger's possible succession to Rogers, Stewart Alsop wrote: "As the West's dependence on Middle East oil increases, so does this country's interest in promoting a Middle East settlement. Any settlement the Arabs could conceivably accept would be bitterly resisted by many Israelis and American Zionists. But the first Jewish Secretary of State in American history could not easily be charged with promoting an anti-Jewish policy."[2] "Officials realize," Peter Lisagor reported soon after his appointment, "that Kissinger's ability to appear evenhanded in his dealings with the Arabs may depend upon how skillfully he handles the question on military supplies to Israel. [Officials] recall that former Secretary of State William P. Rogers also established a rapport with the Arab leaders, but could not in the end overcome U.S. policy of aiding Israel to keep an arms balance."[3]

Astonishing though it may appear to future historians probing the relation of Jerusalem to its vaunted friends and pro-
tectors in Washington, on the eve of the October War the
conventional wisdom in Washington regarded its Israeli friend
as recalcitrant and obstructive and its foe as reasonable and
cooperative. There is every indication, both from private and
public utterances then and later, that Kissinger shared the conventional wisdom in Washington. Washington's notion of a
Middle East settlement had earlier been formulated in terms
coincidental with those espoused in Cairo and Moscow—most
notably in the so-called Rogers Plan of 1969—but Washington
could not quite deny enough military and other support for
Jerusalem to undermine American diplomatic designs. The frustration that was setting in with the growing realization of Rogers'
futility was tinged with resentment—and not without grudging
respect—for the little Israeli tail that was wagging the big American dog.

It was probably inevitable that, as the Russians confidently
assumed even while the June War raged, sooner or later Washington would seek another rapprochement with the Arabs at
Israel's expense. But the degree of ideological *Gleichschaltung*
with Cairo reached some time in the aftermath of that war, not
just in the State Department—where it is less surprising—but
even beyond and especially in the press, is indeed astonishing.

There were unprecedented circumstances behind this remarkable development: for one, their crushing defeat of the Arabs
in the war suddenly deprived the Israelis of their sympathetic
"little David" image, which the media quickly transferred to the
suddenly rediscovered Palestinians; for another, shocked by
their dismal press in the West in the prelude to the war and immediately thereafter, Arab sources initiated an effort toward
better public relations abroad, chiefly by suppressing much of
the genocidal agitation that most offended foreign sensitivities.
Henceforward even the *fedayeen* would not always tell Westerners that they sought to destroy the Jewish state, but rather
that they aspired to a "democratic and secular" state, which is

the same thing but sounds much better and even means different
things to Westerners. It was becoming socially acceptable, even
fashionable in some circles, always more so among the liberal
and sophisticated than in the general public, to be openly anti-
Israeli. This climate of opinion ensured the success of a bold
Arab and Soviet venture in United Nations politics and psychological warfare.

When the Soviet war-scare in Syria and Nasser's subsequent belligerent maneuvers—chasing the United Nations Emergency Force out of Sinai and Gaza, reimposing the naval block-
ade at Tiran, and marching his armed forces to Israel's borders
in coordination with other Arab forces and with threats to destroy her—had backfired in the devastating Israeli strikes on
June 5 and after, the losers set out to have the world wipe out
the consequences of their ill-fated adventure. (The battle-cry in
the Arab world in the aftermath of the war urged "elimination
of the traces of Israeli aggression.") They quickly summoned
the United Nations to an emergency session and Kosygin came
to Glassboro to demand from President Johnson immediate
Israeli withdrawal from conquered territory. That the United
Nations would actually endorse the gist of this maneuver, by
forces that had just defied it, became immediately apparent; it
had in fact been a foregone conclusion as far as those more
intimately aware of the organization were concerned. Students
of the organization and increasingly even the lay public had long
become thoroughly accustomed to its systematic anti-Israeli bias.
But with the genocidal threats still ringing in their ears, the
delegates to the Assembly could not quite allow endorsement
of the essential Arab demand in its crude form; a sufficiently
large number felt it would be outrageous to do so, holding out
for a more ethical version. As participants in these events later
explained, there was a growing feeling that, if Israeli were to be
asked actually to take the extraordinary step of restoring the
losses of those who had just promised her death, it ought at
least to take place in a context of peace.[4] Hence the idea of
"withdrawal," which had never been in doubt from the first in

that organization, came to be "balanced" with the idea of "peace," and was to be linked with it in one way or another in the various resolutions and rhetoric in the United Nations.

In view of the fact that by repetition of this linkage there has arisen in our minds something of an equation, as if these ideas were synonymous and interchangeable, it is important to insist on what did *not* happen when the linkage took place. The United Nations did not scramble to avert war and, having investigated the conditions of peace in the Middle East, came up with withdrawal as essential. In fact, when the Soviet-Arab maneuvers had plunged the world into crisis in May of 1967, and fears of war rose daily, anxious Western delegates could not get the Security Council even to sit and talk for long, much less to act on the crisis. (A majority agreed with the Soviet, Arab and allied delegates who argued that there was no crisis— Israel then seemed on the run and worse, in danger of being overrun by Arab might.) The United Nations moved to act only when asked to bail out the ill-fated adventure, was in fact summoned because it could be counted on to do so. What it addressed was demand for withdrawal, which it endorsed as expected, but with the proviso that it take place in a context of peace. Whether peace was at all possible in this generation or whether withdrawal would bring it nearer or further delay it was not pondered in this purely political act.

By the incessant repetition of the linkage of "withdrawal" and "peace" in diplomacy, the press and private discussion generated the conditioned reflex in which one automatically thought of both when hearing either. Richard Pipes termed this Pavlovian event one of the grandest confidence schemes in recent history. (In effect, the Russians had pulled off one just like it in the early 1950's with their global peace offensive, when, with less success than now, they managed to link their posture in various international issues with "peace" in the minds of millions around the world.) The confusion reached the point where pressing for withdrawal meant struggling for peace, and viceversa. In the "newspeak" prevailing in much of the public discourse on the Middle East it became commonplace for, say, an Arab diplomat to express his confidence in continued American pressure for Israeli withdrawal by casually saying that America's interest in "peace" had not waned under the new President (Omar Saqaf, after his first meeting with Ford); and the media and the public at large automatically saw Kissinger bringing peace to the Middle East with his achievement of Israeli retreats, as in the disengagement pacts on the Egyptian and Syrian fronts.

This success emboldened the Arabs to extend further the substitution of partisan claim for universal desideratum, in two stages; the first, aimed at making "withdrawal" synonymous with "total withdrawal," achieved considerable success, in great part because of the carelessness and ignorance with which even the serious press handled this vital distinction. As students of this conflict know, the operative clause on withdrawal in the crucial Security Council Resolution of November, 1967 ("No. 242") reads in the authoritative English version (having been sponsored and drafted by the British) "from territories occupied in the recent conflict." The omission of "the" before "territories" was not accidental; it represented the outcome of an intense struggle between the Arab-Soviet bloc and American-led forces anxious to prevent an Israeli rejection of a resolution barring any and all territorial adjustment. (The Rogers Plan two years later settled on only "insubstantial" adjustment.) Between no Security Council resolution on withdrawal and a less than perfect one, the Soviet Union and the main Arab forces in the struggle opted for the latter, but continued to cite it always as if it required withdrawal from all lost land. In the United States the media referred to this essential matter only rarely with some indication of awareness, almost invariably dropping or picking up the "the" as casually as random usage would have it in connection with any other part of speech. Analysis of *The New York Times* revealed not only frequent use of the false version (it was standard in the reporting by Bernard Gwertzman and others), but sometimes even its use in quotas, as if citing the resolution verbatim.

In the second stage the popularized shibboleth appeared increasingly linked to claims going beyond even total retreat to the armistice lines existing before the 1967 war. This took the form of some mention of either the "rights" or "national rights" of the Palestinian "people" or "nation" in addition to "withdrawal." A more ambitious maneuver than the former, this linkage was made with greater frequency since the October War, when the likelihood of obtaining just "withdrawal" suddenly increased to near certainty in Arab eyes.

The 1974 American diplomatic offensive that so excited and gratified the Arab world was not the first with which Kissinger was associated. Contrary to popular belief, he was involved also in the first Middle East campaign of the Nixon presidency, that started in the fall of 1968 even before the formal assumption of office and petered out two years later. Kissinger had assumed a "low profile" for this area of policy, because of his reported anxiety over the implications of his Jewish origin and out of simple expediency—the need to give visibility to Secretary Rogers, presumably the President's chief foreign policy adviser, in at least one part of the world. Kissinger's National Security Council was not cut off from Middle East policy; though he remained in the background he conferred with Arab and Israeli officials; he gave no indication of dissenting from the policy and actually explicated it in off-the-record sessions and was from time to time cited as stating it in terms even stronger than the Secretary himself, as in the widely publicized briefings in late June of 1970 at San Clemente. The chief of Kissinger's Middle East staff, Harold Saunders, on at least one public occasion endorsed the policy and expressed confidence in its success, at Princeton, on June 5, 1969. Upon Kissinger's succession to Rogers, Saunders also moved to the State Department and Joseph Sisco, who as Rogers' chief aide for Middle East policy, worked closely with Kissinger, was elevated to chief political officer of the whole Department (Undersecretary for Political Affairs).

The diplomatic offensive launched by Nixon had the earmarks of the "linkage" strategy which Kissinger was said to pursue in his policy: it sought to tie in a Middle East settlement with a balance of great power interests. Through a process of systematic consultations the great powers were to produce an

agreed outline of a settlement to be put to the Arabs and Israelis for implementation. What was in fact produced was quite
different. To start with, Nixon's frequent description of the area
as a "powder keg" about to trigger a global explosion—his
rationale for the offensive—in effect produced something like
hysteria in the media and the public at home and immediately
heated up the situation in the Middle East. To give substance
to the anxieties abroad in the West, President Nasser launched
his war of attrition along the Suez Canal. At home, the media
and the politicians led the public in following excitedly and nerv-
ously the publicized meetings of the Big Four ambassadors in
New York and the more mysterious têtes-à-têtes between Sisco
and Soviet Ambassador Dobrynin in Washington, whence was
to arise the formula for saving the world from the Middle East-
erners and the latter from their destructive compulsions. The
Big Four meetings were a simple sham, in which the two super-
powers merely humored British and French pretensions to great
power status; between the great powers there was played out a
more intricate sham, passing for negotiation, with the United
States producing a succession of increasingly conciliatory proposals for settlement, the Soviet Union invariably expressing
satisfaction with the concessions and, making none of its own,
encouraging the United States to go back and try harder still,
which it invariably did. The American side thus managed to
negotiate with itself throughout 1969 and, having compromised
the negotiating posture of its Israeli protégé almost entirely, was
told by Moscow and Cairo it was on the right path, but still
some distance away from the right place.

When the American proposals were made public as the
Rogers Plan at the end of the year, it turned out that all these
labors had produced a near carbon copy of the bankrupt formula imposed in the aftermath of the previous war, in 1956.
While protesting strenuously that they would not repeat that
fiasco, the American side came up with the same total (or near
total) Israeli withdrawal from conquered territory in return for
an ambiguous Arab pledge of peaceful intent (not to be a peace
treaty) and the United Nations presence and international guar-

antees that in the past never worked when needed. Like the proverbial Bourbons, they seemed not to forget anything, nor could they learn from history. Israel rejected the American proposals furiously and, successfully resisting pressure to bow, signaled the plan's at least temporary demise. In a post-mortem to the grand offensive, Peter Grose, a journalist who had closely followed it concluded that American policy makers had indeed managed to be dead wrong all along as far as the real posture of their own ally was concerned.[3]

American intervention further managed to precipitate a deadlock also in the United Nations mediation effort, entrusted to Ambassador Gunnar Jarring of Sweden. When, following several rounds of consultations in the Middle East, at the United Nations and elsewhere for over three years, Jarring finally put his proposals openly to Egypt and Israel, he asked the former to aver readiness to conclude a peaceful agreement ultimately and the latter to accept total withdrawal from the Sinai prior to negotiations. Israel had already rejected this condition in the Rogers Plan and Egypt was, if anything, less willing than before to settle for less, now that the United Nations mediator endorsed the American position. This action eliminated completely what useful role Jarring might still have played, but it is easy to see that, with the United States joining the other permanent members of the Security Council in asking for complete withdrawal from the Sinai, the United Nations mediator was emboldened to ask no less. In any event, after Jarring had thus played himself out at the start of 1971, Rogers sought to fill the void with the promotion of a scheme for an Israeli pullback from the Suez Canal zone. The scheme had first been floated by Moshe Dayan and seemed acceptable to the Egyptians, but was stalled by the latters' insistence on the same demand from Israel that had killed the Jarring mission. The conviction was spreading that Israel's posture had to be broken, if peace was to come to the Middle East.

At the outset of Nixon's second term a new American diplomatic offensive in the Middle East seemed in the making, with the looming energy crisis and Sadat's overtures to Washington (chiefly by the "expulsion" of Soviet military personnel from Egypt in the previous summer) adding some new incentives. Pondering this possibility, Leslie Gelb, a former high defense official for policy planning, suggested that the thing to watch out for would not be change in the substance of American policy so much as the mode of the change.

"If the past gives any indication of President Nixon's future style," he wrote, "he will try to change Middle East policy in sudden and sweeping fashion. My guess is that the President will think about his moves in the Middle East in much the same way as he approached altering China policy. Until the dramatic public announcement of his impending visit to China, Nixon and Kissinger controlled all the contacts with Peking themselves, shielding not only the public but their bureaucracy as well. Their fears, so it seems, were twofold: (1) that the bureaucracy would urge caution and pacing (go slow) and insist on prior consultations with our Japanese allies: and (2) that the bureaucracy in order to ensure its advice would be taken would leak the secret Washington-Peking contacts to the press, thus alerting all of the domestic political opponents of deserting the Chinese Nationalists, thus endangering the whole opening to the Chinese Nationalists.

"This China model for breaking new ground would seem to apply to Israel as well. While there is no particular love for Israel in the national security bureaucracy (albeit the U. S. military does admire Israel's military prowess), a sufficient number of Foreign Service Officers and military men do look upon Israel as an ally, with all of the allied rights of consultation and information. Nixon and Kissinger, therefore, would again be concerned about press leaks. And while their fears of a renascent China lobby may have proved groundless, there can be little doubt in their minds that the Israel lobby would raise a storm of protests about too sudden a reconciliation with the Arabs—especially a reconciliation the substance of which would be known only to a handful of men.

"Thus, the Nixon-Kissinger method of changing Middle East policy is likely to be prolonged, closely-held secret negotiations with heads of Arab states (if Sadat and others are prepared to play that game) followed by a dramatic public announcement. With some justification, Nixon and Kissinger seem to believe that the only way to hurdle the many domestic political and bureaucratic obstacles to change is to get as much as possible done privately and then confront the outside world with a *fait accompli*.

"The substance of these secret exchanges probably will fall into four areas. First would come the resumption of diplomatic relations with the Cairo Government. Second would follow some kind of economic aid program—but not military aid which President Nixon might urge our European allies to provide. Third, there might be some form of an arms limitations deal with the Soviet Union on types and quantities of weaponry to be provided to Israel and the Arab states. Fourth, a campaign of public rhetorical and diplomatic pressure might ensue, revolving around Israel's agreeing to return most, if not all, of the occupied territories, including as an immediate step an Israeli pullback from the Suez."[6]

(Anticipating more recently a new policy for Cuba, William Safire wrote: "If you were to handle it Kissinger-style, you would order up a top-secret National Security Council memorandum; you would dispatch your national security adviser to a secret meeting on a fishing boat within sight of the lights of Havana; and you would announce on national television, with a mystery guest standing in the wings puffing a large cigar, that you have ended the threat ninety miles from our shores that plagued three previous Presidents.")[7]

President Nixon soon announced that the Middle East was indeed high on his agenda for the second term. He designated Henry Kissinger to succeed William Rogers late in the summer and the new Secretary of State took the oath of office on September 22, 1973.

6. Tilting Toward Whom?

Henry Kissinger made his formal approach to the Middle East with a bang.[1] Only two days in office, he spoke in the United Nations of America's "special obligation" in the search for a Middle East settlement and announced we "are prepared to use our influence" and even "to urge" toward that end.[2] The Egyptians had in the same words been urging all along to acknowledge such a duty. To Arab delegates he declared afterward "the United States understood the Arab concern over the current Middle East stalemate, and asserted that it was necessary 'to find ways' of creating a situation 'with which you can live.' "[3] The Israelis were preparing for "Kissinger's winter offensive," but here the Secretary denied harboring any "very dramatic moves," and asked the Arabs not to expect him to bring "miracles."[4] But he was to do just that within not many days, once the Arabs attacked Israel in great force. As the fighting was ebbing, Kissinger explained to Mohammed Hassanein Haikal in Cairo, "you made it possible for us to perform a role we desired to perform and felt ourselves capable of performing."[5]

When three years earlier Kissinger said: "The United States is committed to defend Israel's existence, but not Israel's conquests,"[6] the waves this caused agitated many here and abroad for some time afterward. While one could view that as just a more ruthless expression of Administration policy on the territorial question, one could also—from an Arab perspective— view it as an invitation to attack Israel. Making a distinction between Israel's existence and Israel's conquests in war is fatuous for, regardless of Arab intent, ground war was bound to start at the "conquests"—the occupied territory—and Israel's one defense force had to fight—and could be destroyed— wherever war was waged. Even Arab attacks on Israel "proper," by air or from the sea, were to be directed at an Israel in a state of disgrace—holding "conquered" territory. The only practical effect was to exonerate an Arab attack in advance. And when the attack actually came, in October of 1973, Kissinger indeed at his press conference on October 25, 1973, at the Department of State, sought to excuse it on just such grounds.

It is reasonable to assume, as many have, that Kissinger did not anticipate the Arab attack in October and was in fact surprised and alarmed by it, for many reasons. Sadat had cried wolf too often in the past to be believable as a warrior; such an attack would be suicidal, besides; the Russians would henceforward abstain from mischief for the sake of détente. That Kissinger misjudged the intent of others is less disturbing than his apparent unawareness of the danger in his statement.

The Administration's launching of the previous diplomatic offensive in the Middle East had been taken by Egypt as the signal for heating up the conflict, to underscore and dramatize the urgency of the matter. As was widely understood at the time, Nasser was waging his "war of attrition" to keep the powers alarmed and busy trying to get him a settlement from Israel. The fact that his losses in lives and material were enormous did not matter, if that purpose was served. Sadat after him repeatedly said he would risk terrible military defeat to heat up the Middle East for the same purpose, and he significantly termed his October attack "Operation Spark." The theme was in fact what informed much of the Arab consciousness in the years after the June War. For the Secretary and his advisers not to have pondered gravely the likelihood of Sadat "assisting" Kissinger in his urgent initiative or getting him to try harder—after waiting for him for so long—would seem to border on the incredible, suggesting either reckless disregard of Arab political behavior or simply ignorance of it.

When the war began, hardly anyone in Washington thought it would take too long for Israel to crush the Arabs; certainly less than the famous six days of the last time. The judgment was not much more wrong than official judgments in previous confrontations between the Middle Eastern antagonists. Having predicted that the Arabs would quickly push the Jews into the sea in their first war in 1948, American officials persisted in the assumption that the Israeli "edge" must be fading, even though the subsequent wars, in 1956 and 1967, indicated that it was, if anything, widening still further. When the officials finally inclined to abandon this belief, nearly before the 1973 war, there was neither conviction nor real conceptual shift in their thinking. Foreign policy leaders and professional military analysts had only a tenuous belief in Israel's military superiority, based on technical considerations such as the quality of her material, while academic students held a firmer view of Israeli superiority, one based on analyses of both Israeli and Arab societies and actual warfare. Thus when the fourth war came, the assumption in Washington was that, in view of the Soviet advisers' "eviction" from Egypt a year earlier, Israel had to crush the Arabs more quickly than in the last war, a view shared by the incoming Secretary of State. Since this failed to materialize, a new view quickly took hold in the same quarters, which, projecting fortuitous circumstances in this war as permanent in future wars, instead regarded Israel as sinking. Now the "supersabra" gave way to an equally mythical "new Arab," —rational and technically competent. The Secretary was remarkably active in spreading this prophecy of doom, as in the December 6, 1973, meeting with Jewish intellectuals, and justified his Middle East policy by it. (Pressing Israel for far-reaching territorial and other potentially jeopardizing concessions on the ground that she is anyway ultimately militarily indefensible is not new, and was in fact the policy of other Secretaries of State before Kissinger, most notably John Foster Dulles.) None of the academic experts who undertook systematic studies of the long war in the Middle East supported this view; those who examined and commented on the events of the last encounter, in October of 1973, agreed that no substantial change in the warfare capacitres of the two sides was manifested.[7]

The October War produced an almost unique convergence of advantages for the Arabs. They attacked with enormously large forces lines that were virtually undefended, so that the coincidence of overpreparedness and underpreparedness produced on the Syrian front a confrontation of some 1,500 tanks with 70 on the other side, while the mass of the Egyptian army, having trained in every detail for many years for just this operation, encountered in all some 600 Israelis in crossing the Suez Canal as the defenders of the Bar-Lev Line on the east bank. (The Bar-Lev Line, misrepresented as a replica of the Maginot Line, was more aptly described by Israeli troops as "Swiss cheese with more holes than cheese.")

Moreover, the Israelis had on this occasion conceded the initiative to the Arabs, and quite deliberately. Arab preparations were known; the likelihood and, at a later point, the certainty of attack were clearly appreciated in Jerusalem. But the Israelis refrained from launching pre-emptive strikes or even mobilizing their reserves, for a combination of reasons. Secretary Kissinger had strongly urged the Israelis to desist and the good will of Washington, particularly on the eve of uncertain and dangerous developments, weighed very heavily in their deliberations. Strengthening such decision was the Israelis' own reluctance to appear as an aggressor in American and other foreign opinion, allowing the Arabs to strike first for all to see. It was the unprecedented sense of security derived from the wider and strategically superior borders acquired in the last war that enabled them to contemplate a defensive approach on this occasion. The level of Israel's toleration of Arab provocation or threatening military moves had drastically risen in the wake of the June War. Whatever the diplomatic and public relations cost of preemption, there is no doubt that losses would have been minimized, even though heavy losses of aircraft would have been sustained, the force of Arab attack reduced, and the morale of the foe adversely affected. As it happened, most governments, under the threat of an oil boycott or already committed to the Arabs in advance, accused Israel as the aggressor; whether an Israeli preemptive strike on such huge concentration of Arab forces poised for attack would have much affected American sympathies is questionable.

In addition, the Israelis suffered heavy losses in tanks and aircraft from the surprising appearance of advanced Soviet arms in vast quantities on the battlefield. An essentially technical problem to which answers are found in the realms of technique, this had an immediate devastating effect on Israeli warfare, in encumbering its offensive, mobile capacities while strengthening the kind of sedentary, attritional warfare that Arabs, not congenial with a modern war of movement, are only able to wage well. The unplanned attrition in turn quickly depleted Israel's stock of munitions and other "consumables," adding yet another critical aspect to her condition. While the Arabs were constantly re-supplied by their foreign sources in the ensuing orgy of destruction, the Israelis faced the trauma of depleted reserves without assurance of new supplies throughout the entire first week of the war. Washington did not move to replace Israeli losses until the eighth day of war and other foreign suppliers refused altogether, London actually violating an agreement with Jerusalem on spares for arms. The ensuing floundering in the Israeli military command further aggravated the errors and misfortunes.

Under such optimal conditions, that the Arabs found themselves soon facing a military debacle possibly no less devastating than in the past suggested some trenchant judgments on the nature of the continuing military disparity in the Middle East. But that was clearly not the evaluation that conformed to American policy for the area; instead, the suitable one was Kissinger's dictum, that the Jewish state was "finished" militarily, as he told the Jewish intellectuals soon after the war.

But two days into the war, beginning to hurt badly, the Israelis turned to the United States with urgent requests for certain items of ammunition and spare parts and the accelerated delivery of aircraft promised to them long before the war began. Israeli Ambassador Simcha Dinitz expressed to Secretary Kissinger his country's feeling that, having entered the war at great disadvantage after the latter's warning against preemption, they expected America to shoulder a special responsibility to assist them with equipment. Although Kissinger immediately promised help, the Israelis were kept waiting unsatisfied; increasingly urgent requests for more varied and larger amounts of arms were equally stalled, except for a trifle. Urgency reached crisis on October 10, when Israel's needs exceeded mere replacement of aircraft and short items, requiring total logistic support on such a scale as to render all but a massive American airlift inadequate. A massive Soviet airlift and sealift to both Egypt and Syria had already been under way for several days. Facing the awesome likelihood of unilateral disarmament in a raging war, the Israeli military were drifting, unassured of sufficient supplies for an offensive and unable to escape the further attrition from protracted, stationary warfare. The airforce was curtailing operations and the stocks of ammunition were nearing such low points that heavy casualties were suffered for lack of firepower. By the 12th of October the situation was becoming desperate for Israel, but apart from a series of stillborn schemes and a trickle of supplies which a few El Al aircraft could carry to Lod in Israel, no American aid was forthcoming. On the next day, the eighth of the war, a vast American airlift to Israel was suddenly started.

Why so late?

An explanation furnished by Kissinger portrayed him working energetically and incessantly from the first for full, speedy satisfaction of Israel's requirements. Although backed by the President, he claimed to have been frustrated by Secretary of Defense Schlesinger and his aides, who succeeded in defying the wishes of their Commander-in-Chief and his chief foreign policy adviser for nearly a week. In this the Pentagon was motivated by concern for oil supplies from the Arab world, the Deputy Secretary of Defense, William Clements, being represented as the oil industry's man in the defense establishment. So tough was the struggle, according to Kissinger, that he was not sure he could pull off another such feat for Israel, especially since he saw Congressional support for her to be waning.

An elaborate and authoritative presentation of the Secretary's version may be found in the Kalbs' affectionate biography, *Kissinger*. It is a fascinating story, with Dinitz invariably coming to Kissinger with worries and requests and leaving, if not fully reassured, at least with the sympathies and ever new ideas for success the next time, of a struggling ally, the Secretary of State. Kissinger is portrayed consulting with Dinitz on schemes and techniques for meeting Israel's increasingly more desperate needs. Kissinger pleads with Schlesinger; cajoles, argues and threatens on the phone, in the presence of Dinitz; arranges for meetings with Dinitz. There appears to be an almost endless series of dashed hopes; promises die unfulfilled; elaborate plans for supplying Israel collapse over small details or last-minute snags. The end is elusive. Kissinger fights Schlesinger in a "one-man fight" for days, only to discover suddenly that it is Clements who is the real obstacle. Now one must start all over again, it seems. Then, just in the nick of time, as Israel faced catastrophe and her Washington envoy announced the desperate step of taking his case to the streets, Kissinger succeeded in clearing all obstacles. Thus ends, in victory over the oil lobby and the generals, the plight of a tormented ambassador and his friend and ally at State.

President Nixon was not heard in public on these critical events, other than to claim credit for "saving" Israel in the war in his struggle against ouster from office, as repeatedly reported by Rabbi Baruch Korff, who rallied support for him in that struggle. Secretary Schlesinger consistently denied opposing Kissinger on the Israel re-supply matter. "Your suggestion," he replied to a journalist's query, "that the Department of Defense was seen to be dragging its heels in re-supplying Israel is wrong; there is a difference between dragging your heels and having your shoes nailed to the floor by national policy. Also wrong is any suggestion that the Defense Department was slow in im-

plementing the charter [of commercial cargo planes] policy and
that I was admonished by Kissinger for not taking charge of the
re-supply effort. I don't recall any such thing. It strikes me as
preposterous."[8] Kissinger joined in Schlesinger's denial of a rift
between them in this matter,[9] but did not attempt to reconcile
the inconsistency in his own statements, nor did the press pursue
the matter further.

This writer's early inquiries in March of 1974 into the
October events in Washington revealed little disposition among
individuals intimate with the foreign policy making process to
treat the Kissinger version seriously. While differences were acknowledged between the chiefs of State and Defense on re-
supplying Israel, as on many other matters, they were said to be
of an entirely different nature from the clash in the Kissinger
version, frequently termed a "fairy tale" by these informants.
The version they reported reversed the role allegedly played by
the Secretary of State: some said Kissinger himself opposed re-
supplying Israel, even against the wishes of Schlesinger; others
said Kissinger had the acquiescence of Schlesinger, albeit not
for so long as he himself sought to deny aid to Israel. In both
variants, however, Kissinger did not fight for re-supply, but actually led the fight against it. When, as already mentioned, Leslie Gelb later casually referred to this version as Washington
lore in an essay in *The Times*, on April 21, it caused hardly a
ripple in either the Capital or the media.

A public elaboration of Washington's open secret followed
in the summer, in an article by Tad Szulc which upset popular
beliefs concerning other actions also by Kissinger in the October
War. "Schlesinger favored in principle a re-supply airlift flown
by American military aircraft," he wrote, "but he was paralyzed
by a White House policy directive, drafted by Kissinger, ordering a hold on such operations. The written directive was a Kissingerian masterpiece of devious diplomacy. Its thrust was that
the Pentagon would be represented to the Israelis by Kissinger
as the 'bad guys,' refusing help, while the White House and the
State Department would appear as the 'good guys,' fighting a
bureaucratic battle to aid Israel."[10] Szulc's probing revealed the

vaunted peace-maker and healer in a somewhat different role in October. "For two weeks, Kissinger refused to launch serious diplomatic efforts to bring a Middle East cease-fire on the theory, according to insiders, that a long-range political settlement would be facilitated if both the Arabs and the Israelis made each other suffer. . . . As in the case of Vietnam, he concluded that political solutions can be obtained in otherwise intractable situations only after a period of high-intensity fighting."

But Kissinger sought to extend the agony—which was Israel's alone, since the Arabs were amply aided from all sides— long past the point at which Schlesinger and Nixon felt they wanted to play the game. According to Szulc, Secretary Schlesinger informed Kissinger on October 12, that the only solution for the Israelis was an American military airlift. Since a massive Soviet airlift was bringing supplies to Egypt and Syria, he felt that the United States was no longer obliged to exercise restraint. Besides, the Israelis were thought to be in desperate straits. Yet Kissinger still sought to prevent the airlift. While the Pentagon was already getting the airlift under way, Kissinger told Dinitz that it was continuing to block the operation. Kissinger then produced various notions which were rejected by the Pentagon, since their effect would have been either to delay or encumber the airlift. One notion would have involved flying the cargo to an American Air Force base on one island in the Portuguese Azores, whence it would be taken by boat to another Azores island, to be picked up from its commercial airport by El Al airliners. Even if there were time for such an operation, there were no boats available for it in any event. Early on Saturday, October 13, Nixon ordered Schlesinger to commence the American airlift. Since Portugal had not yet authorized the refueling at the American base in the Azores the huge C-5 cargo jets and the C-130's flew nonstop from the United States to Tel Aviv, carrying more fuel and less cargo.

As for the startling worldwide alert of American forces ordered on October 25, which Kissinger suggested was triggered by ominous Soviet military moves and diplomatic behavior, promising to explain the matter more fully later, Szulc detected traces of consistency with Kissinger's actions earlier in the war. Top intelligence officials told Szulc there was nothing to indicate that the Russians were preparing to invade the Middle East; if anything, they may have been pulling together a force for the enforcement of the cease-fire jointly with an American force, as requested by Sadat. But only 60 soldiers in civilian clothes were sent to Egypt as observers when Washington disagreed; an equal number of Americans were dispatched to Israel on a similar mission. According to State Department officials, Kissinger used the reports of Soviet military moves to scare the Israelis into observing the cease-fire. He had just joined with the Russians to stop the fighting when Egypt appeared on the verge of military collapse. Later Kissinger ordered a meticulous study of the events that precipitated the alert, presumably in preparation for the promised explanation, but the project was quietly dropped when it developed that no convincing material was available.

A little over a year after the alert, Thomas Ross reported from Washington that intelligence officials denied the Kissinger version flatly. According to them, "the technical intelligence did not indicate that the Soviets intended to intervene directly with troops in support of Egypt."[11] Then, Ray Cline, former director of State Department intelligence, himself repudiated Kissinger's handling of this affair, in the Winter 1974-75 issue of *Foreign Policy*.

The contradictory versions of the airlift crisis were submitted to rigorous scrutiny by Edward Luttwak and Walter Laqueur, who concluded that the Kissinger version must be rejected as "highly implausible."[12] In view of the fact that Kissinger was then in firm control of foreign policy, as both the President's National Security Adviser and Secretary of State, more so than any of his recent predecessors, excepting possibly John Foster Dulles, only the strongest evidence would suffice to persuade anyone that Schlesinger could so blatantly have opposed the President's "foreign-policy czar," especially since the President is said to have supported Kissinger all along. Yet no such evidence has been presented. The role supposedly played by Clements is deemed incredible on similar grounds. "The Nixon administration, then still a living creature, was noted for its high degree of centralization; it was a regime in which no Deputy Secretary of Anything could oppose Presidential policy in the manner portrayed by the Dinitz-Kissinger version of the crisis. He would have been out in a matter of hours." What external evidence there is, conflicts with that version, Luttwak and Laqueur citing two instances: as for internal evidence, they found the story to be inconsistent with itself, to boot. "While discounting the elements of personal animosity in both versions, it seems most plausible that the main obstacle to a rapid flow of military supplies to Israel was not Schlesinger, let alone Clements. It could only have been Kissinger." The Insight Team of *The Sunday Times* (London) reached the same conclusion in their book, *The Yom Kippur War*, 1974.

The American airlift gave Israel the material and psychological boost to turn on her attackers with decisive moves. Having already checked the Syrian onslaught on the Golan and pushed the allied Arab armies there—including Iraqi, Jordanian and Moroccan—to the outskirts of Damascus, the Israelis now moved in strength to the south, where the Egyptians, having crossed the Canal and failed to advance in the Sinai, had dug in typical hedgehog fashion close to its east bank. In a fashion characteristic of them, the Israelis had been contemplating a daring and fast moving operation aimed, in the last resort, at the jugular of Egypt's armed might. Operation Gazelle was launched on October 15 under the command of General Ariel Sharon, quickly breaking through the Egyptian lines in their weakest link and crossing the Canal, established a bridgehead on the west bank. The speed and unconventionality of the offensive did not merely surprise the Egyptians, they actually seemed unable to grasp its meaning until it was nearly over. The Commander in Chief of their armed forces, General Ahmed Ismail, stated that he knew nothing about the offensive until a full day later and even then he was told that only a small force of 7 tanks had come across the Canal.[13] Meanwhile the Israelis were roaming behind the backs of the bulk of Egypt's armed might entrenched on the other side of the waterway, moving with lightning speed northward to Ismailia, southward to Suez City, taking out the Soviet missile batteries, destroying enemy forces and installations as they advanced, and fanning out westward, where Cairo lay only a short distance away, virtually undefended. With the Egyptian command still euphoric over the successful crossing of October 6, in their heartland proper there took shape an awesome re-enactment of the debacles of the past. The Israelis were about to entrap the whole of their armed force on the east bank (2nd and 3rd Armies); on the west bank booty and prisoners were breaking faster than they could take them; the road to Cairo was free for the taking. A week after the American airlift began, Egypt faced a disaster comparable to the catastrophic Russian defeat at Tannenberg (in World War One) and seemed not even to be aware of it.

But the Russians were aware of the ominous turn of events. They had joyously egged on the Arabs to expand the war, calling on all Arab nations to join the Egyptians and Syrians and their allies; they had greeted with acclaim the embargo on oil shipments to the United States and other western nations, initiated on October 16 as punishment for the airlift and pressure for wider Arab goals, urging still more harm for their partners in détente. A flood of Soviet arms and spares to keep the Arabs fighting had been in motion virtually from the start. But the way the war was going now, it had to be stopped, and quickly. Kosygin rushed to Cairo to make the Egyptians realize the fullness of the impending disaster. Kissinger was "summoned" to Moscow (the term was actually used in the press reports) and immediately departed and quickly joined the Russians in putting a halt to these developments. The cease-fire order was endorsed by the Security Council in New York in the early hours of October 22.

In the rush of events and the elation over an end to the war, there was hardly any contemplation in the United States of other consequences or interpretations of what was happening. Here the failure of the press is so complete that the public is not aware of it; the earlier elaborate trail of reporters after the peripatetic diplomat, with its role confusion and identification with him, and the consequent substitution of his definitions of foreign affairs for theirs had resulted in one unchallenged meaning of the Moscow mission. But the European allies, despite their admittedly craven submission to the oil threat—and possibly because of it, for they, unlike the United States were fundamentally vulnerable to it—viewed this mission as yet another nail in the Western coffin. They saw Kissinger as assuring the effectiveness of the oil weapon. The Arabs (and their Soviet allies) had put a gun to the head of the Western nations—one that would not vanish if allowed to stay—but Kissinger was not even trying to use the gun the Israelis had put in *his* hands.

" 'Oil supplies from Saudi Arabia and the Gulf would be back to normal very soon,' an European Economic Community official said [afterward, following disengagement at Suez] 'if America could tell the Arabs that Israeli forces will stay on the west bank of the canal until the embargo is lifted, and that they will be allowed to return if it is reimposed. But Kissinger threw this ace away at the outset of the game, even obliging the Israelis to trade a territorial advantage in order to secure an exchange of prisoners to which they were entitled anyway.' "[14] The concensus of E. E. C. foreign ministries was that the Russians would not have sent troops to chase the Israelis out. (In the United States it was erroneously claimed that Kissinger had so precipitously responded to Moscow's request because the latter threatened drastic measures, when in reality this happened only after the cease-fire.) The American press never really explained the tension between Washington and our European allies following the October War, except to speak rather vaguely of failure of consultation concerning the Middle East problem.

If there was toughness in Kissinger, it was reserved for others. The Israelis reacted to the cease-fire as if struck by lightning. As they saw it, they had suffered a sneak attack on the most sacred of their holy days and managed to blunt it only with a terrible cost to them in young lives; now the powers intervened to protect their tormentors from retribution. All their horror was to be for less than nothing—to leave the Arabs triumphant. Many sensed a more profoundly ominous meaning in it that touched on their very survival. But the immediate, practical consideration was the consequences of freezing a daring operation: unfulfilled, the ingredients of success turned into grave liability. What in a matter of days could achieve total victory became a mass of extended and exposed lines in a distant and vulnerable bridgehead, a drain through attrition on the national economy and on lives. That the Israelis should have wanted badly to achieve at least one objective, as a chip for bargaining their way out of this mess, clearly followed. Their government felt it could not defy the order in principle, but also that it would have to ignore it in practice, at least for a while. They would have sought to circumvent the cease-fire in any event, but the Egyptians appeared to have obliged them by failing to observe it themselves. (The Israelis appeared rather to count on this unwitting cooperation ever since the Egyptians obliged them in this fashion in the October offensive in the Negev in their first war, in 1948.) The chaotic disarray in much of the Egyptian army at this time would surely have made some firing on the foe inevitable in any case. In the ensuing two days of warfare, the Israelis surrounded Suez City and trapped the whole of the Egyptian 3rd Army on the east bank of the Canal.

Kissinger's efforts after Moscow were directed chiefly at stopping the Israeli offensive and rescuing the encircled Egyptians. Arriving in Tel Aviv on October 22, from the Soviet Union, he managed to allay some anxieties concerning the integrity of Israel's bargaining posture in the negotiations envisaged by the cease-fire resolution. The firing was renewed on October 23, triggering a whirlwind of American diplomacy: Ambassador Keating rushed to make "serious representations" in Tel Aviv as Ambassador Scali rushed to issue another cease-fire order at the Security Council on the same day, culminating in the still mysterious world-wide military alert soon after midnight on October 25. The explanation most widely accepted by Washington officials at this time held that Kissinger overreacted in typical fashion in his fear that the Moscow deal was coming unstuck, then used the panicky step to further intimidate the

Israelis (as well as to make a show of firmness toward the Russians at home).

The Israelis would not easily relent on the encircled Third Army, even if they stopped advancing any more, thus sparing the Second Army to the north. But unless the trapped forces were soon furnished most urgently with water and medicine, they would have to surrender, an event the Sadat regime could probably not have survived. The fear and fury in Moscow made the Israelis deeply anxious, yet not enough to loosen the noose. The Russians had reportedly warned the Israelis, the Americans relaying the threat, that they would themselves undertake to deliver the requirements of the encircled Egyptians if the trap was not broken. In the end it took an extraordinary American act to break the Israelis' resolve, according to Moshe Dayan, then Israeli Minister of Defense, who said that Kissinger demanded that the Israelis allow unconditionally the provisioning of the Third Army. He threatened that the Israelis would be left to face alone a Russian intervention if they did not comply, adding that he himself would proceed to rescue the Egyptians, using United States aircraft for this purpose. The State Department, without denying it, refused to discuss his allegation further.[15]

part four
The Disengagement Pacts

7. Achievement vs. Ballyhoo

His management of the October War occasioned for Henry Kissinger perhaps the greatest personal successes of his career. The crucial maneuver was the denial of supplies to Israel and in this the control of one individual was vital. For so long as Dinitz could be persuaded that supplies for his country would be forthcoming by working with Kissinger, he would refrain from taking his case to the Congress and the public. It was unthinkable that supplies could be denied if the American people were aware of the situation; indeed, when Dinitz finally threatened to break from Kissinger, one week later, supplies suddenly started flowing to Israel.

In his handling of Dinitz, Kissinger showed remarkable skills at manipulation. He ingratiated himself with the Israeli Ambassador, appearing invariably sympathetic to his country's needs and fears and flattering to her envoy. As with reporters, he presumed to a fallacious sense of solidarity, and with similarly deleterious results, as Dinitz, too, tended to identify with the Secretary. For the basic ploy, Kissinger resorted to what Luttwak and Laqueur termed the "Mutt and Jeff" police routine, playing the friendly cop, who endeavors to help the mark, victimized by another cop. The bad guy was Schlesinger; Nixon, as usual, was the benevolent but distant presence in the background. With the Jewish refugee become the Emperor's minister struggling against oil-minded tormentors of his people, we have a plot fit for the popular Yiddish stage, in essence an updated Purim play.

In staging, playing and improvising the plot Kissinger displayed much ingenuity and resourcefulness. At one point, when Dinitz showed signs of wavering, it occurred to Kissinger to have a special telephone installed in the Israeli Embassy—a "hot line" for Dinitz. The plot had to be improvised almost daily, so a variety of plans for getting supplies to Israel appeared one after the other, all terribly complex and esoteric, sufficiently promising to engage Dinitz for a day or two, then certain to abort, making room for yet another, and so on. When Schlesinger's "Haman" required additional plausibility, William Clements was brought into play; as a Texan connected to the petroleum industry, he lent himself well to the role of spoiler.

Kissinger could count on the sympathetic cooperation of players and bystanders in Washington, where the climate had turned increasingly antagonistic to Israel's resolute stance on negotiations with Arabs. As indicated earlier, Israel appeared to much of the foreign policy community as the main obstacle to a settlement that the looming energy crisis made seem increasingly urgent. Whatever the full or real intent behind the anti-Israeli act, it could be interpreted in this and similarly positive terms. One popular theory held that the Arabs had to gain some self-respect on the battlefield before they could start negotiating with the Israelis. The theory was attractive for several reasons: in the first place, it made support for such an act seem almost pro-Israeli, since peace is said to be Israel's chief objective. (Could a member of Congress endorse such a policy unless so explained?) Moreover, the theory sounded expert— for is it not known that Arabs are particularly emotional, proud and inordinately much concerned with "face"? Thus it seemed shrewd to give them just enough satisfaction on the battlefield to enable them to proceed to the essential job of settling with Israel. It is of course true that the Arabs craved even a semblance of martial success, but why this should dissolve their rejection of Jewish statehood was not clear. It was there *before* the humiliation of the battlefield that presumably stood in the way of peace. That is the stuff of which much of the foreign policy folklore is made, and the theory affected real events in that critical situation. Yet another form in which the anti-Israeli act appeared positive was to view it not as giving the Arabs victory, but rather as merely preventing a too crushing defeat for them. Since their earlier debacle was seen as having only hardened the stalemate, another one could be expected to freeze it permanently.

Kissinger's success hinged on his ability to restrict the drama to high-level diplomacy in the exclusive circles supportive or acquiescent of moves that broader American opinion would reject. The Israelis could only be led, not coerced, into staying there, and, having already followed his lead into the war, tended to follow him further. Staying with him in the airlift crisis then made following him into the cease-fire more probable still. (By now the Israelis had "built up" a psychological investment in cooperating with Kissinger.) When Kissinger then came to extricate them from the lingering pain of his cease-fire, at their expense, their dependence on him deepened further.

The "what" of his management of the October War is as characteristically Kissingerian as the "how." If the latter reveals him as clever manipulator, the former shows him in typical warrior posture. When in war, Kissinger's inclination is not to rush to put out the fires, but rather to use them to further his purposes. One must recall that Kissinger displayed a rather casual approach to war (indeed, nuclear war) at the start of his political career, in the 1950's as adviser to Nelson Rockefeller, which made him for many the personification of Dr. Strangelove. As chief foreign policy adviser to President Nixon, his interventions in various armed conflicts have impressed students of international affairs as brutal. "Kissinger's temptation to brandish the Bomb—first elaborated in *Nuclear Weapons and Foreign*

Policy—is sometimes irresistible," Ronald Steel recently wrote.[1] The Christmas 1972 terror bombing of North Vietnam emerges from Szulc's probe of the cease-fire negotiations as a supererogatory, if not wanton, exercise in violence. Then there was the dispatch of an aircraft carrier to the Bay of Bengal in the Bangladesh War; the full-scale nuclear alert in the October War; the less publicized beginnings of another Cuban "missile crisis" earlier, in 1970, when the Russians appeared to be building a submarine base in that island.

As characteristic as the big stick is the "tilt." It was Jack Anderson's revelation that gave us a first candid glimpse of Kissinger at war. Behind a facade of benevolent neutrality, concern and compassion appeared a warrior in mufti ordering his staff to "tilt" energetically toward the "Paks" (who were slaughtering Bengalis by the tens of thousands daily). When the Greek military junta overthrew Makarios, Kissinger did not rush to quench the flames, accepting the Sampson regime in Nicosia and failing to dissuade the Turks from invading the island, indeed continuing to supply them as they fought another American ally. And in the October War, earlier, he had worked hard to deny America's friends critical supplies for as long as he could—even as they suffered grave losses—only to labor just as energetically to deny them the fruits of their victory, once they recovered.

The problem of "why" is in foreign policy almost always unnecessarily encumbered by a quite theological habit. The statesman is rare whose purpose is not "peace" and ubiquity of the abstraction empties it of meaning as motive, even if sincerely adduced. But the familiar suggestion of peace as the purpose of statecraft is reinforced by a popular misconception of the process of foreign policy. As Daniel Patrick Moynihan reminded us, politics is not to be confused with the process of scientific inquiry. This does not mean that policy makers are indifferent to peace—peace is often ardently desired by them— but that their actions in pursuit of peace are not governed so much by dispassionate study of the nature of conflicts as by the weight of pressures on them. While not incurious as to the nature of conflicts they encounter, policy makers do not probe them as, say medical researchers probe illness—in order to unlock the paths of therapy. Rather, they maneuver the vector of forces within the framework of conflicts and hope that this brings peace nearer.

Although some may have academic backgrounds, the foreign policy makers' perspective is diplomatic, not scholarly. Their imagination of problems derives in essence from conversations, chiefly with other policy makers. This may at times produce shrewd insights, but as a method has no necessary or even probable relationship to reality. That is what scholarly researchers are about, assuming that they do their work properly. Thus they would think of chances for peace in the Middle East in terms of Islamic conceptions of war and international order, the status of Jews in the Muslin tradition, or the political significance of Islam, rather than in relation to what President Tito or Secretary Brezhnev may be saying, as policy makers are more likely to do. Policy makers are more aware of the *decisions* concerning the Middle East than what their or lasting impact on the area may be. An illustration is furnished by the earlier cited Security Council Resolution 242, representing a parliamentary accommodation in the United Nations, but taken as a blueprint for Middle East peace in subsequent diplomatic activity. Whether in fact this compromise (not between Israelis and Arabs, incidentally, but between wider and varied blocks) bears any such relation to the stated objective seems hardly to concern the diplomatic actors.

Writing as an academic student of international relations, in *A World Restored* and elsewhere, Kissinger himself argued that peace could not be made the goal of foreign policy; rather, it had to be seen as a bonus flowing from a well-conceived policy. As practitioner, he has lately demonstrated the sophistic potential of this presumption. Referring to his moves in the Middle East, he urged against ideal visions of peace, asserting that peace is the diplomatic process itself.[2] What Kissinger does *is* peace. This equation of self with peace is only consistent with the intense personalization of American foreign policy and the confusion of his career, perceptions and needs with it.[3] But it at least helps us look for the "why" of United States policy in the October War.

8. Who Wins, Who Loses?

The new Secretary faced a remarkable convergence of pressures, the common denominator of which was that they could be satisfied at Israel's expense (and other Jewish interests). As a man reputed to possess a considerable ego, craving success and—as Nixon recommended him to the Arabs—unaccustomed to failing, Kissinger could obtain movement and the semblance, if no more, of breakthrough by pushing Israel and substantial achievement through tangible concessions from her. Previous American diplomatic offensives were denied such success in the last resort precisely by Israel's refusal to grant them.

Kissinger's chief had parallel needs. With his regime on the edge of the Watergate abyss, Nixon frantically sought all the more diversion in foreign affairs. Besides, the Middle East impasse seemed the last unfinished business in his grandiose ambition for "a generation of peace," as his legacy to the world. There was a deep yearning in him to add to his grand historical "opening" to China and Russia also one to the "one hundred million Arabs," as he proudly reminded us in his farewell address. He could still save his place in history as peacemaker, but the Israelis, for whom he had done so much, were less than forthcoming. In a press conference, just two months before nominating Kissinger to State, Nixon took the unusual step of blaming Israel for the stalemate. (He also blamed the Arabs, of course, but the point was not lost on observers.)

To these pressures was added the rising anxiety over oil. Spot shortages of gasoline in the summer had given a taste of the more terrible things to come, predicted in a steady stream of ominous words from Arab sources, oil company executives and, increasingly, government officials. We can save ourselves, their message invariably read, only by acting against Israel (working for a "settlement," in one version, or being more "even-handed," in another, or plainly forcing Israel to withdraw, in the more frank statements). By summer's end, Washington informants privately advised callers that the Administration, while publicly rejecting any connection of energy to Israel, was about to get rough with her. A former colleague of this writer came away from talks with White House aides with the distinct feeling that the Israelis had better prepare themselves for a real trauma.

America's European allies, who had since 1967 steadily increased their distance from Israel under French guidance—a process America not only failed to check, but actually enhanced by adopting in 1969 the French "big four" approach to a Middle East settlement—were increasingly acting to convey Arab pressures on the United States. Paris had been softening Bonn, London and Rome to the point where Cairo could openly orchestrate them in pressures against Washington. American support of Israel was thus made a source of disunity within the Atlantic alliance, besides isolating the United States in the larger international community. It appeared that one could alleviate both also at Israel's expense.

Not least, there was Russia, the character of Kissingerian détente requiring that Israeli (and other Jewish) coin redeem both the competitive and the cooperative aspects of the relationship to Moscow. Nixon (with Kissinger's concurrence or at his initiative) dramatically defined the Middle East as the most likely point of ominous superpower confrontation and moved immediately upon assuming office to seek accommodation with Moscow, to "defuse" the Arab Israeli conflict. The process necessarily involved compromising Israel's negotiating posture, even though no agreement with Moscow resulted. Any mollification of Moscow required some weakening of support for

Israel. Preventing the break-up of détente over the Middle East merely added urgency to the Administration's desires for a settlement nobody thought was attainable without substantial Israeli retreats.

The fact that Kissinger shared the conventional wisdom on the Middle East supports the growing consensus of students of international affairs that he is conceptually unimaginative and conformist.[1] Few could evaluate him better in this regard than his Harvard peers, and even his loyal friends among them failed to claim intellectual creativity for him. When his bestseller, *Nuclear Weapons and Foreign Policy*, appeared, he was widely accused of borrowing ideas hatched by others, without giving them credit.[2] Ralph Lapp, the military analyst, termed the book "a great mascara job," for Kissinger was using ideas that were specious to boot, as he himself later conceded. Donald Brennan, formerly president of the Hudson Institute, said of Kissinger's work at the Council on Foreign Relations, which sponsored the book: "He was serving as *rapporteur*. Naturally, in that setting, he would pick up ideas from others. He's very bright and witty but his talents are primarily political." Others agree, but think the ideas were primarily acquired outside, mainly from Bernard Brodie and Edward Teller. Referring to Kissinger's Harvard days, one source said: "He was very smart but not a creative thinker. He soaked up other people's ideas so well, perhaps unconsciously. . . . [Which] led a lot of people here to feel that Henry was fundamentally superficial."

Kissinger's ideological substratum thus supported and rationalized his opportunistic imperatives. Neither was the Administration prepared to jeopardize détente over Jewish emigration from the Soviet Union and Kissinger openly led the fight against the Jackson Amendment linking American concessions in trade to freer exit from the Soviet Union. Here the Kissinger argument was similar to his ominous analogy of the Middle East to the Balkans that had sparked a world war once before: besides constituting illegitimate meddling in Soviet domestic affairs, demands for Jewish emigration actually jeopardized the world's peace.

But the Secretary was no less concerned about the growing Soviet presence in the Middle East and this anxiety was given appropriate expression in his widely-quoted assertion of the need to "expel" the Russians from Egypt. "While in many ways a master of subtlety, Kissinger is remarkably crude in his approach to power politics," observed Ronald Steel. "It is the strong opponent who counts, and every event is judged by its relation to the current struggle for dominance among the great powers. Just as the revolt of the Bengalis and the thirty-years old war in Vietnam were seen as part of the cold war, so in the Middle East it was Moscow's 'penetration' of the area that troubled Kissinger, not the tiresome quarrel between Arabs and Jews."[3] And Sadat had already signaled his readiness to play in the summer a year earlier, when he sent the bulk of his Russian advisers out of the country. The "expulsion" ploy, too, had to be played at Israel's expense; above all, Kissinger had to demonstrate his readiness to "deliver" the Israelis. As reported by Philip Ben from Brussels in *Maariv* (June 5, 1974), in talks with European diplomats after the war, Kissinger has referred to his achievement in deflating the Soviet Union in Arab eyes as one of the great events of the 1970's, warning that he would not let the Israelis jeopardize that success in any way.

(This orientation made it even less likely that Kissinger's intervention in the struggle of Arabs and Israelis was guided by the realities of the conflict and the actual desiderata of accommodation or even peace between them. How his obsession with realpolitik can unhinge his touch with reality has been indicated by Steel in relation to the more recent Cyprus crisis, where his actions appear also to have nothing to do with the root problem, the old hostility between Greeks and Turks. His tendency to "paper over" real conflicts has been noted elsewhere. If other reasons have not already made the reliability of Kissinger's evaluations of the progress of peace between Arabs and Israelis questionable, this certainly should.)

But the Israelis were not about to oblige their American friends. This defiance of patron by client was in itself a drastic innovation in international relations since 1967. The pattern of American-Israeli relations before had been obvious and predictable: Jerusalem could not resist for long American pressure and often complied with alacrity. It was American pressure that restored to Egypt territory lost in wars with Israel each time, in 1949 and again in 1957. For a variety of reasons, this was not repeated in the immediate aftermath of the June War, chiefly because the Johnson Administration felt that precipitous intervention in the past merely helped to perpetuate the conflict and because the Israelis were more determined to resist such intervention after yet another war. Few believed that Israel would resist American intervention that subsequently developed, taking toward the end of 1969 the form of the Rogers Plan, envisaging virtually complete evacuation of conquered territories once again. But by 1971, with the plan still on paper, students of international relations were for the first time contemplating seriously a substantial Israeli capacity to ignore dictation from the United States. They spoke of a new era in international politics, in which clients manipulated patrons, rather than the other way around, with tails wagging dogs, for a change, and patrons in bondage.

The novelty could be easily explained. Once Jerusalem was determined really to resist Washington dictation, the latter faced the painful resort of punishing a client to the point of endangering its survival—assuming that domestic opinion would tolerate such punishment in the first place. Hence the peculiar post-1967 relationship, with Washington at odds with Jerusalem on the crucial territorial issue among others, yet seemingly unable to deny Jerusalem for long the military and economic assistance which helped the latter to continue resisting its benefactor. Combined with a sense of military might and economic boom, the new political posture infused Israel with unprecedented confidence. On the eve of the October War, the notion of an Israeli "paramountcy" in the whole Middle East had become quite current in discourse on the affairs of the region. If Kissinger was to obtain compliance with his wishes, he was not going to get it from a confident Israel.

Thus the surprising thing is not that Kissinger seized the opportunity early in the October War to weaken Israel, but rather how far he wished to push her, though Nixon and Schlesinger felt they had gone far enough. In light of the subsequent blustering imposition of the cease-fire and the efforts at spreading defeatism and gloom among America's supporters of Israel, one must conclude that her trauma fell still short of Kissinger's expectations. But it was more than sufficient for him to harvest the greatest success of his career.

The spectacle of America's Jewish Secretary of State descending from the war into the enthusiastic embrace of Arab leaders could not but stun his countrymen. But the Arab leaders certainly knew what they were doing. To grasp their perception, one should try to step into Sadat's shoes for but a while. The meaning of a prompt resupply of Israel's forces in October could surely not be lost on the Egyptian, or other Arab leaders; or a failure to stop the Israelis in the third week of the war. The Americans had bled the Israelis (the notion that Kissinger made both sides suffer is nonsensical, since attrition is the Arab strategy and pretty much a way of slow death for Israel); then he proceeded to stave off military disaster and possibly the fall of the regime in Cairo. He promised, moreover, full restoration of Arab territorial losses, or so Sadat tells everyone he meets. He assumed the deferential stance of the properly chastened transgressor, vowing never to allow America to outrage the Arabs, as in the past, and acknowledging that the latter had indeed forced America back to the right path. Yet the meaning of "October" for the Arabs went far beyond this, for that signified for them ascendancy on a magnitude comparable to the great Muslim conquests thirteen hundred years ago. If Kissinger did not bring it about—and no Arab would accept that—he certainly played midwife to the miracle, born of oil and martial triumph (for that is how Arabs viewed the war). Had they been crushed yet another time by Israel, who knows whether there would have been more than futile rage left behind the oil weapon?

For his countrymen, the spectacular descent on Cairo was but one in a series of stunning achievements. The Russians were said to have lost Egypt to the United States. One after the other, previously hostile Arab leaders were seen scurrying to the side of the American. Formal relations with many Arab regimes were to be renewed soon. The logjam in the ancient conflict itself appeared miraculously to break, as Arabs and Jews were under Kissinger's guidance moving gingerly toward accommodation for the first time. We were told of sensational turnabouts in the Arab's attitudes, now suddenly accepting Israel and yearning for the peace that his vision could make real. The Arab officers could be seen on American television screens daily talking to Israeli officers at Kilometer 101—and was this not unprecedented, the very thing the Arabs were said to have obdurately refused to do for a quarter of a century? Moreover, under Kissinger's aegis these ancient belligerents were actually to go to a peace conference at Geneva. There was a revolution also, we read, on the other side, where Israelis were finally emerging from the clouds of their myths and fallacies, freeing themselves from the shackles that had kept them from facing the reality of the Arab world and from necessary accommodation. Shuttling between them, Kissinger unlocked their minds and hearts to one another, interpreting each to the other, blending their deepest fears into mutual aspirations. It was too much to expect from any man—and even a year later the foreign affairs specialist, Holbrooke, felt he had to plead with the people to recognize that Kissinger "is far from a god."[4] It was too good to be true, yet there seemed little, if any, doubt that it indeed was. (One would be hard pressed to trace in the contemporary press any mention that, for instance, the presumably unprecedented military talks under U. N. aegis at Kilometer 101 were in effect the typical Arab-Israeli contact virtually throughout the whole of their conflict.)

But the very summit of success were the disengagement pacts produced in the stunning shuttling diplomacy between Middle Eastern capitals soon after—"one of the great pieces of modern diplomacy, a technical triumph of awesome proportion," a fairly typical expert evaluation (by Holbrooke)[5] held while the media and the public at large simply termed the events miraculous. Here the country was presented with an indeed unprecedented spectacle, a drama in which the stakes were seen as no less than war or peace; the hero, truly the Lone Ranger in the popular imagination, patiently and doggedly chipping away at the forbidding block of ancient hostility, and slowly and brilliantly drawing at first, merely the hopeful outlines of an impossible dream, then fleshing it out to loom as exhilarating possibility virtually within his grasp, only to stumble within a step or two from the goal. But he would not retreat, even against all odds, trying again and again. The people were naturally absorbed, deeply involved. Who knows how many millions had come to identify strongly with the hero, feeling his disappointments and sharing his pride? Then, after cliffhangers and nearly exhausting suspense, the release of a triumphant ending. If the first performance in Egypt was fabulous the replay in Syria bordered on the fantastic.

Never before had a diplomatic achievement been seen to be so great by so many, yet few acclaimed diplomatic feats were so much of a sure thing as this. For on closer scrutiny of the substances of the negotiations, the stunning achievement appears in making the virtually inevitable seem miraculous. Perhaps none grasped this unusual talent of the man so well as Art Buchwald, in an essay on Kissinger as husband. Asked by his new wife to fetch two loaves of bread at the market, Kissinger never actually produces them; there is plenty of bread there but this very fact makes him envision "problems."

"He returns in a half-hour. 'What kind of bread did you want, rye or white?'

" 'It really doesn't matter, Henry. Either one will do.'

" 'It's not going to be that easy. The supermarket has more white than it does rye and therefore they have put the white bread up in the front and the rye bread in the back. They're demanding guarantees that I buy two loaves of white for every loaf of rye. I've taken the position we should have the right to buy the rye bread without having to purchase the white bread.'

Told once again that any kind would do, Kissinger plunges instead into "shuttling" with steadily more complex matters to tackle. "By this time several reporters who are standing outside the Kissinger home surround the Secretary of State. 'Mr. Kissinger,' one of the reporters asks, 'we understand you're trying to buy bread for your dinner tonight. Do you think you'll be able to do it?'

" 'There are still some last-minute details to be worked out,' Henry says, 'but I'm optimistic that there will be a deal.'

"But when Henry returns from the supermarket he is glum and tells the reporters: 'I would be less than candid if I told you that I brought back bread.'

" 'The supermarket has raised some last-minute conditions on slicing that I'm not sure can be met. But after reporting to my wife I am going back and make one more effort to find a compromise which both sides can live with.'

In the end he triumphantly returns with some crackers—not quite what his wife wanted, but a hopeful beginning of a difficult task—to the acclaim of the press. "Henry's done it again."[6]

Troop disengagement was made virtually inevitable by Kissinger's intervention against Israel in the third week of October of 1973. What it made equally certain was that disengagement was something the Arabs would enjoy and the Israelis would pay for. Apart from the hopelessly intertwined frontlines on the Suez Canal that made disengagement imperative, as a rationalization of demarcation and communication lines, there was a much more profound reason, especially for Israel. For Kissinger's stoppage of the war simply meant that Israel could neither finish the war by finishing off the Arabs nor by sending her troops home. So they had to pay a price for the Arabs' permission to let them do the latter. Neither was the Kissinger cease-fire a cease-fire for both sides: the Arabs were free to wage a sedentary war of attrition—the only kind they wage well—while the hurting Israelis were not really free to wage their kind, a modern war of movement. After all, that was "war," and the United States and Russia had stopped war. The same did not apply to the continuing Egyptian (and later Syrian) firing from fixed positions. Thus the only real question was how high a price was Kissinger to extract from Israel for disengagement.

When one looks carefully at the deal, one realizes that the shuttling and presumed brilliant "conceptual breakthroughs" ended in pretty much the same pact the Israelis had been pressing on Egypt long before the October War. That deal proposed an Israeli pullback from the Canal to a distance of several miles against an extended cease-fire, during which progress toward a final agreement would be sought. First floated by Moshe Dayan, the essential idea was accepted by Sadat, and this basic consensus had propelled Washington to seek "proximity talks" under United States auspices to flesh out a deal. Details pertaining to the extent of withdrawal and cease-fire period and size and character of Egyptian forces permitted on the east bank of the Canal appeared not to constitute too much of an obstacle, but the deal got stuck on Sadat's demand that it be linked to a full Israeli withdrawal from Sinai, which Israel rejected.

As for the price that Israel was to pay for the imperative disengagement with Egypt, Kissinger "invented" the Dayan Plan, the additional irony being that Sadat had to go to war to take a deal available to him without one. The fact that he dropped his demand for full Israeli withdrawal for this particular deal after the war was hailed by our foreign policy officials as a great act of statesmanship. But it is difficult to see how he could have done otherwise, given the actual circumstances of Egypt's debacle in the war and the triumph into which disengagement turned it. Taking the deal meant ending the entrapment of his forces and jeopardy to Egypt's heartland and Capital while getting additional Israeli withdrawal in the Sinai as well. Besides, Sadat claimed to have had Kissinger's commitment to extract full Israeli withdrawal anyway. While the American side denied this, many remained doubtful whereas Egyptians and other Arabs certainly acted as if such commitment was indeed in their hands, in any case.

So it took a war to materialize the Dayan Plan, to produce some "movement" for which Washington had yearned so long, but the claim that the war had also softened the essential postures of the antagonists, made immediately and repeatedly by Kissinger and Nixon, was suspect on the grounds that made the Dayan Plan possible. For what had prevented this was Sadat's insistence on a linkage to incompatible ultimate aspirations, and it was not a bridging of them that made it possible, but precisely an effort to ignore them in that instance. From Kissinger's assumptions of the beneficial effects from the pain of war, it would seem to follow that any mellowing *must* occur after the appropriate cure,[7] and the success in pressing the Israelis for additional, more extensive withdrawals certainly depended on whether they and the American people accept this proposition. But to cite the disengagement as evidence for it was surely ironic.

Similarly spurious logic dominated the thinking on the Syrian disengagement pact that followed some four months later. A popular belief, encouraged by Kissinger's entourage, held that such a pact was much less likely than the Egyptian, because the Syrians were not prepared to accept the Jewish state, whereas the former presumably had already passed this hurdle. And when the Syrians finally assented to a pact it naturally appeared to many that Damascus had also passed it at last.

The Syrian pact was never much more in doubt than the Egyptian, the greater difficulty here being technical rather than principle. True, the Syrians were less comfortable with the Americans, and the Israelis less conciliatory toward them, than the Egyptians; but they had dealt with Americans before and made military agreements with Israel as well, long ago, even when contemporary, optimistic evaluations of their stance conceded that they did not accept the Jewish state. A more obvious difficulty in military agreement with Syria derived from the fact that there was so much less to give on Israel's northern front than in the south. The Golan, unlike most of the Sinai, is invaluable for the security of part of the Israeli heartland and already quite densely settled with permanent Israeli residents, besides comprising a much smaller area than the desert separating the Israeli Negev from the Suez Canal.

For the Syrians, who had relatively little confidence in further Israeli withdrawals on the Golan and hardly in full withdrawal, military disengagement appeared as possibly the last chance for getting something from Israel, at least for some time. And since Egypt, Israel, the Americans, and others wanted a Syrian disengagement badly, the Syrians would be fools to give one quickly, rather than linger and extract every possible concession under the circumstances. To be sure, they also held on to their Israeli prisoners of war as a bargaining chip. The tight haggling in a relatively claustrophobic setting conveyed abroad the mistaken impression that principle was at stake, hence the popular belief, rendered emotional by the drama of Kissingerian shuttling and upbeat-downbeat-upbeat press conferences, that something unexpected and well-nigh unachievable had to be pulled off.

On the basis of this analysis, it was possible to anticipate a Syrian disengagement pact with confidence even before Kissinger's shuttling between Jerusalem and Damascus, and in such detail as to match the agreement that was actually concluded, which was in fact done by this writer,[8] among others. The most significant of these was the envisaged concession of Kuneitra to the Syrians; for the desolate and destroyed city had enormous symbolic value for them—its recovery suggests liberation of the province whose center it used to be—whereas the Israelis could give it up with perhaps less pain than any other bit of their part of the Golan. Since the Israelis never intended to keep the salient conquered in October, any Syrian craving for land lost in the previous war could be satisfied only with tiny slivers, with Kuneitra among them at the very least.

It is of particular interest that Egypt's leadership had been remarkably confident in a Syrian deal throughout the period marked here by anxiety and uncertainty. As early as February 9, one of Sadat's close confidants, Abd al-Quddous, published in Cairo's *Akhbar al-Yom* a stunningly prescient scenario of things to come. "Kissinger," he wrote, "deals with Syria in the same way he deals with Egypt. . . . Kissinger has formulated his idea of the lines that will separate the Syrian and Israeli forces . . . This line is identical with the line suggested by Syria. As he did with Egypt, Kissinger intends to summon Moshe Dayan to agree with him on this line. After that, the Geneva conference will convene, Syria will attend it, agreement will be finally reached, and Israel will begin to withdraw in accordance with the disengagement agreement. Israel is opposed to the agreement which is to be reached in Geneva. When this plan is submitted, it will create problems that will compel Kissinger to board his plane to shuttle between Damascus and Jerusalem —as he did between Egypt and Israel." (A report in the Paris *L'Express* of May 27–June 2, 1974, suggested the nature of these "problems," when citing four personal messages from Nixon to Meir during the shuttling urging compliance with Kissinger's demands, the third of these involving the explicit threat to abandon Israel totally in a new war.)[9] Perhaps Sadat knew more than he let out when confidently predicting that his "Doctor Henry" would soon accomplish another "miracle."

part five
Is There a "New" Middle East?

9. Bases of (Mis)Information

Nixon and Kissinger claimed the epochal achievement of securing the first real break in the long Arab-Israel conflict, deemed
the most intractable of all international disputes. Nowhere else,
said Nixon, was America's "unique and essential contribution
to peace" better demonstrated than in that case. "For the first
time in a generation we are witnessing the beginning of a dialogue between the Arab states and Israel. Now, the road to a
just and lasting and permanent peace in the Mideast is still long
and difficult and lies before us. But what seemed to be an insur-
mountable roadblock on that road has now been removed, and
we are determined to stay on course until we have reached our
goal of a permanent peace in that area."[1]

Kissinger, to whom Nixon conceded in public a crucial role
in this triumph, proclaimed the revolutionary shift in Arab attitudes as assiduously as Nixon staked out claims to history's
gratitude. Returning from Cairo soon after the war, he reported
to the Senate Foreign Relations Committee that Egypt gave
every indication of finally closing the struggle with Israel and
that this attitude was spreading in the Arab world;[2] to the press
he announced Egypt's "bold decision to move from confrontation to negotiation as a means of resolving the Arab-Israeli dispute."[3] He announced the historical change to the Israeli public
in Jerusalem, on June 17, 1974, speaking not merely of coex-

istence, but of "friendly acceptance" by the Arabs. More sanguine judgments were made on private occasions; in one, with Jewish intellectuals, on December 6, 1973, Kissinger claimed to have detected the movement toward reversal even before the war.

The press treated this spectacular claim as factual and reported it as an independent source as well. In the immediate aftermath of the war in particular such reports announced sudden and thoroughgoing reversals in the Arab world almost daily. Algeria, it was asserted one day, had drastically changed her position and was now for a "negotiated peace with Israel" as were also the *fedayeen* and others in the Arab world.[4] Egypt, one read another day, had just accomplished an "astonishing shift of position" endorsed by other Arab states.[5] In the news reports and editorials, in print and on the air, there was an avalanche of "recognitions," "acceptances," and similar indications of the end of conflict rolling throughout the Arab world. As far as could be determined, the great mass of the American people remained dubious about Arab intent toward Israel. Seven out of ten respondents believed they were still determined to eliminate the Jewish state, according to a Harris poll right after the war.[6]

In closer scrutiny, those grand claims rested on disturbingly thin ground. Many, like Nixon in the above address, cited the disengagement pacts. "The [Syrian] accord, once concluded," read a typical evaluation, "can be taken as firm repudiation of the old Arab ideology that forbade any notice to be taken that a Zionist state exists in the Middle East. If there are not good relations between Israel and the Arabs, there are at least relations—mutual undertakings, joint ventures in however limited a sphere. A growing acceptance of the fact of Israel has been detected among Arab thinkers ever since 1967; now that acceptance is being codified in a formal agreement."[7] (Editorial comment in the same issue took such a pact to demonstrate "the good intentions of these longtime belligerents.") That this was dubious evidence was quite obvious.

Some of the ground, particularly in news reporting, was simply spurious inference, as was the case also in the above quotation. In *The New York Times*, straight from Cairo, Henry Tanner reported that the acquiescence by Arab states in Egypt's participation in the Geneva conference "implies" recognition of Israel.[8] An editorial in the same newspaper had much earlier averred that "Egypt *in effect* acknowledged Israel's right to exist. . . ."[9] A typical summary of the November summit in Algiers announced that "the Arab states for the first time *tacitly* recognized the right of Israel to exist as a state."[10] Such discovery of new departures was not a recent development at all, even though the latter-day practitioners may not have known it. Thus it was explained that, by not walking out of the United Nations when Israel was admitted in 1949, the Arabs had granted *de facto* recognition to the Jewish State. A quarter of a century later one was told that Arab states had in effect done the same in the aftermath of the October War.

In a report on Syrian disengagement, entitled "A Pact That Could Reshape the Arab World," Henry Tanner claimed that "it has become natural for millions of Arabs to think of Israel as a country like any other." On what grounds? Because, he wrote, the Arab press often quoted Israeli Minister Peres, among others, on the status of the negotiations during Secretary Kissinger's shuttling. The heading for this read "Accepting Israel," no less.[11] On that basis the Arabs could be said to have made their peace with the foe quite a few years ago.

Some claims were obviously wishful thinking, such as the popular belief, launched in the closing days of the October War, that Egypt had finally agreed to direct talks with Israel. The concession seemed particularly important in view of the adamancy with which Cairo had previously resisted direct talks. Then suddenly one learned from Sadat himself that he had not agreed to direct talks.[12] Did we here have an optical illusion or did he perform a demagogic trick to disguise reality from his people? We may have thought the latter, since a "peace conference" denoted just what he denied. But the Egyptians viewed Geneva as an occasion for the United Nations and the great powers to compel Israeli compliance with their demands.[13] They merely agreed to "gather" in the same hall with Israelis and others under United Nations auspices—as Sadat put it. Had they not been doing just that all the time, in New York and elsewhere?

It was words passed in intimate meetings with Arab leaders that constituted the gist of the evidence Westerners thought they had in support of their sanguine announcements. When this writer probed with the ranking National Security Council Middle East expert the grounds for the official optimism in the wake of the October War, it was to secret conversations with such leaders that he alluded in the last resort, for there were in effect no others worthy of much consideration. But what invariably goes on in these intimate meetings is really no secret anymore, for they have proved over the years to be highly ritualized exercises in cross-cultural misunderstandings, particularly in gauging Arab attitudes toward the Jewish state.

Western interlocutors will approach Arab leaders with uneasiness and anxiety because of their public belligerence toward the Jewish state only to find them charming, ingratiating and disarmingly candid—even self-deprecatory—hosts. To be sure, the Arab leaders will give vent to an enormous sense of outrage, to the great hurt that had been done to their people, and will insist on the depth of their feeling and craving for the right. But they emphatically deny any personal hostility to the foe and certainly no evil intent. If only "justice" were done, things would straighten out; after all, have not Arabs and Jews lived as brothers for so long in the past? They hint darkly at ominous developments if that is not soon done. They explain their public belligerence as political necessity, which the worldly and knowing Western diplomat or journalist "surely understands." To prove their freedom from antagonism they confide in their "friend" that, after all, Israel is a fact that they could recognize.

The pattern has varied as to detail and order of elements, but it has been basically the same with Nasser, Sadat and other Arab leaders, because it reflects not personal idiosyncrasy so much as cultural forces. One finds it even in statements by lesser notables for purposes of advertisement abroad, as in public relations efforts for the *fedayeen* in the American press. In an advertisement in *The New York Times*,[14] an Arab philosophy major explained "Who Are the Palestinians," dwelling first on the outrage done to them. Yet he and his people are free of evil intent toward their tormentors—"we certainly don't wish to do to the Israelis what they did to us." He even expressed sympathy for the Jews' plight in many parts of the world and insisted only a "humane" solution would do. But unless this comes, there will be interminable bloodshed ("no matter how long it takes"). The goal was unexceptionable, "one which enables Israelis and Palestinians to live together in peace"; more precisely, "in the context of a non-sectarian and democratic state which will enable *all* of its inhabitants to develop intellectually, culturally and spiritually." Though he was only an image in words in print, it would have been difficult to dislike this man, who had just used charming words to insist on the destruction of the Jewish state in the major newspaper of the city with the world's largest Jewish population.

We know of the remarkable impact on Western diplomats and journalists of exposure to Arab personal charm. Nasser, who is now said to have been obsessively hostile to Israel, presumably as opposed to Sadat, had in fact as little difficulty in persuading Western visitors of his freedom from such compulsion as Sadat himself. This, not just with amateurs, but even the Arabists of the American foreign service and intelligence operatives, who were persuaded and based national policy on that conviction. As for the usual stream of dignitaries on study missions, journalists and others, they invariably came away either shaken in their earlier belief of Nasserite hostility or persuaded of the opposite. A member of the entourage of President Tito, Leo Mates, who was close to Nasser, explained to this writer that, far from being hostile to Israel, Nasser actually was virtually concerned for her good fortune—though he obviously could not publicly announce this. The tendency of visitors has been to discount even overt hostile acts afterward, having been made privy to the "real" attitude.

Politeness, hospitality and decorum are deeply rooted in Arab culture and, as sociologists have shown, are necessary counterweights to the distrust, hostility and violence that permeate it. Because inter-personal relations are endangered by conflict, the pressure is strong for avoiding conflict in face-to-face encounters, or disguising it by vagueness and pleasantries. An impression of agreement has usually been conveyed where no agreement in fact has existed. The Arab sociologists Sania Hamady and Hamed Ammar, and the Western sociologist Morroe Berger, have explored these dynamics in their works.

The graciousness of Arab hospitality is captivating. Throughout the British rule of Palestine it was common for government officials, policemen or soldiers to turn pro-Arab almost as soon as they arrived in the country, not on political grounds so much as on personal sympathy. The same was true for the civilian and military officials of the several United Nations teams after the establishment of Israel, most of whom, assigned between Jews and Arabs, preferred to live among the latter. Personal sympathy often turns to political bias; after serving as neutrals in the area, many of these men took up in their home countries a militant pro-Arab public position, some becoming full-time activists. When one encounters evidence of unwholesome intent by individuals one really likes, the tendency is to resolve this "dissonance" (as social psychologists term it) by discrediting the evidence (it isn't "true," or when authenticity of statement is unchallengeable, "they don't mean it"). Hence the perennial practice of State Department "Arabists," missionaries and members of the American and British residential colonies in the region (those who "know" it) to apologize for Arabs. The ancient missionary roots of this posture are still manifested by the patronizing quality of this expertise. This is demeaning for Arabs. For instance, it is unfairly implied that, like children they are not to be taken seriously when making objectionable statements—either because "Arabs just are that way," or because their language presumably entices them to utter things they do not mean to say. Those who know Arabic well reject this as a myth. When it does occur, exaggeration on the part of Arabic-speakers may be caused by the necessity to stress the meanings they wish to convey, but certainly not what is *not* intended. Or they are supposed to demand the destruction of Israel only as a bargaining ploy—on the unrealistic assumption that they are merely haggling—as if Arabs, alone among all God's creatures, were unfit to harbor real, honest and genuine antagonism.

Misunderstanding may occur over the Arab resort to subtleties of expression in connection with anxiety-producing issues. For example in order to avoid the use of "Jewish" in relation to their struggle with the Jewish state, they frequently tend to substitute such terms as "racist," "exclusivist," "clerical," "undemocratic," "artificial," "Zionist." Hence to "democratize" or "secularize" Israel (or to "humanize," "de-Zionize," "de-colonize," "normalize" it or turn it into a genuine "Middle Eastern state") means to destroy Jewish statehood. There exists, moreover, a popular belief that Arab messages for foreign consumption are more reliable than Arab messages for Arab publics. But what they say among themselves should not be dismissed out of hand; it must be understood. When one carefully compares Arab messages for foreign consumption with those intended for Arab publics insofar as Israel is concerned, one is struck not by the difference between them, but rather by their similarity, except that those for foreign consumption are less explicit, less precise and less complete. Sometimes the same things said in both the domestic and the foreign contexts are variously interpreted. Thus Arab leaders will insist at home and abroad on the imperative of a "just" settlement, and their followers will instinctively understand that what is meant is ultimately the elimination of the Jewish state.

The most difficult problem in communication is one of which few are aware: the inadequacy of experience in the Western context. The Arab civilization is not a variant of Western civilization but a radically different one in respect to basic concepts, values, mentality and behavior; each making sense in its own, very different, terms. Explaining one such difference, Sania Hamady wrote: "Social control in Arab society is based largely on shaming; hence it depends on primary and close groups in which everyone knows everyone else's acts. In contrast, the members of 'guilt societies' will be constrained, even among strangers, to live up to their moral code of behavior because of their conscience."[15] Thus quite apart from the difficult enough problem in verbal communication there are pitfalls in evaluating Arab intent outside the autochthonous context. This touches on the crucial matter of war and peace, as Harold W. Glidden explained:

"The problem, as the non-Arab sees it, is how to establish peace between the Arabs and Israel; it is felt that time is of the essence. Westerners consider peace to be high on the scale of values, and conflict is deprecated. We also have a highly developed consciousness of the value of time. But on the Arab scale the relative position of the elements is quite different. Overriding is the emotional need for vengeance to eliminate the ego-destroying feeling of shame. Peace is secondary to this need, which is why one often gets the impression that in the Arab context peace is merely the temporary absence of conflict. In fact, in Arab tribal society (where Arab values originated), strife, not peace, was the normal state of affairs because raiding was one of the two main supports of the economy. Even in Islam, itself, the ideal of permanent peace was restricted to the community of Islam and to those non-Muslims who accepted the position of protected persons and paid tribute to Islam. . . . As for the element of time, the Arabs consider it to be of little account in the quest for vengeance, which to them is an integral part of what they conceive of as 'justice.' "[16]

10. On the Spot

If the Arabs changed their attitude toward the Jewish state, they certainly succeeded in hiding this shift very well. There was no letup in their vilifaction of the foe or in the affirmation of his imperative removal. If anything, in private as in public, in speech as in print, at home and abroad, Arab consciousness displayed even greater determination and more confidence than before in the ultimate success of the great struggle.

A careful study of the press of Egypt, the country said to pioneer the drastic shift of position toward Israel, disclosed no such change whatever soon after the October War. Israel remained the quintessence of evil. In a typical statement, she was damned as the fount of aggression, racism, imperialism and more.[1] Or, "The banner of Zionism is the banner of aggression." "The Jews can live in the Middle East if they want but they cannot do this as Zionists." Sadat was quoted as follows: "This struggle is as old as our Arab nation. It goes back to the days of the struggle against the Tartars and the Crusades. . . . Today we fight Zionism in order to protect our rights, our territory and our values."

Not only were there no indications in the immediate aftermath of the war that the struggle with Israel may have been about to end, but the peace conference itself was presented as just one phase in an ongoing struggle whose conclusion lay

farther in the future. The Algiers summit that backed Egypt's
Geneva strategy declared: "The Arab world is passing through
a decisive stage in its history. The struggle against Zionist invasion is a long-haul, historic responsibility that will require still
further trials and sacrifices."[2] The end of the struggle was indicated as coming only with the end of all the outrages that
spell "Zionism" in the Arab world.

Putting this off as either bargaining ploy or rhetorical
flourish will not do, for we have here the gist of the familiar
Arab stance. "The Zionist invasion," Sadat had explained
earlier in a speech to the nation, on June 10, 1971, "will not be
ended with the return of our conquered lands. This invasion has
gone on during our generation and will go on during the life-
time of our children as well. Israeli aggression will continue
even after the most urgent task has been accomplished, which
is the liberation of the land." Or, in an address to the National
Council, on June 2, 1971, "The Zionist conquest to which we
are being subjected will not be terminated by the return of the
occupied territories. . . ." One begins to divine that the in-
nocuous assertion by the Arab heads of state at Algiers to the
effect that so long as "aggression" exists there cannot be lasting
peace in the Middle East, means that Jewish statehood and lasting peace are incompatible. In the Arab usage the idea of
Israeli aggression never requires the commission of a specific
act, since the very existence of the Jewish state *is* aggression.
One grasps even more the pitfalls of communication with Arabs
in realizing that "occupied territory" refers not only to lands
lost in 1967, as is generally assumed here, but to all land held
by Israel before. As Radio Cairo explained, on March 17,
1968: "The real Palestine problem is the existence of Israel in
Palestine. As long as a Zionist existence remains even in a tiny
part of it—that will mean occupation. The important thing is to
liquidate the Israeli occupation, and there is no difference between the territories lately occupied and those occupied before."
The understanding is the same even in Arab countries long
considered close to the West.

On this side of the water the Egyptian attack in October
was widely explained as aimed just at recovering the Sinai and

Secretary Kissinger expressed his sympathetic understanding for this. In Cairo's *Al-Ahram* a man known to speak often the mind of Egypt's leadership gave quite another motive: "The issue," wrote Mohammed Hassanein Haikal on October 19, 1973, "is not just the liberation of the Arab territories occupied since June 5, 1967, but strikes against the future of Israel more powerfully and in a more profound manner, although this is not obvious right now. That means that if the Arabs are able to liberate their territories occupied since June 5, 1967 by force, what can prevent them in the next stage to liberate Palestine itself by force?" Have we here mere flippancy or expression of national policy? These words have precise meaning in the Arab context, where the connection between the recovery of territory and the whole of the Arab cause has been the center of concerns and discussions since 1967.

Whereas in the United States the vaunted Security Council Resolution 242 was believed to outline a final and complete settlement of the Arab-Israeli conflict and thought to be accepted by the Arabs as such, this was in fact never the case. In the Arab world "242" was understood to be addressed only to the losses suffered in 1967, not to the cause of Palestine. For Egypt the problem was "liquidating the results of the June '67 aggression [recovery of territorial losses] without losing sight of the aim of liquidating the results of the aggression of May '48 [establishment of the Jewish state]."[3] The Palestinian *fedayeen* were meanwhile free and able to shoot straight for the latter goal. In one of many such instances, Nasser referred to the *fedayeen* on January 20, 1969, in the National Assembly, "They are entitled to reject this resolution [242], which may serve the purpose of eliminating the consequences of the aggression carried out in June, 1967, but is inadequate for determining the Palestine fate."

The two-stage policy followed by the Arab states since 1967 has conformed more or less closely to a line first put forth by President Bourguiba of Tunisia, who argued that Israel is more vulnerable to peace offensives than to war offensives. "What I propose," he explained after his sensational tour of the Arab world in 1965, "is the application of the United

Nations resolutions; that is, the one about partition [1947] which would permit restoring to an Arab Palestinian state an important part of the territories now occupied by [Israel], and the one concerning the return of the refugees. . . ."[4] It will be up to Israel to reject conciliation or accept it by agreeing to negotiate on the basis he had indicated. The fact that even extreme concessions by Israel on the issues of territory and the Palestinian refugees would not be sufficient was recognized by Bourguiba; the shift he was urging was merely tactical. Even this was resisted at the time, for the lures of a fell swoop removal of the then tiny Israel with utterly indefensible borders could hardly be resisted by most in the Arab world, though the formal stance before the world was already inspired by a strategy of stages. "The official Arab demand," wrote Bernard Lewis in a remarkably prescient passage in 1964, "is no longer for the immediate destruction of Israel but for its reduction to the frontiers laid down in the 1947 partition proposals—obviously as a first step toward its ultimate disappearance. Since Israel, clearly, would not submit voluntarily to such a truncation, and since the Arab states alone are unable to enforce it, this amounts in effect to a demand for an imposed settlement by the great powers—a kind of compulsory surgery on the conference table, in which, perhaps, Soviet arms would wield the knife, while Western diplomacy administered the anaesthetic."[5]

In adopting its two-stage strategy in the aftermath of the November 1967 Security Council resolution, Egypt gained a tactical flexibility that would stand her in good stead in the ensuing years. "Egypt risks nothing," argued Haikal, "by attempting first of all to solve the first phase by political means. The same does not apply to Israel. If the Arabs wish to retract their agreement to the Security Council resolution, it is easy for them to do so by a single word. But if Israel should wish to retract the implementation of this resolution, it will have to fight a new war in order to occupy again the territories it will have evacuated in accordance with the resolution."[6] Thus, Egypt's declared readiness, in February 1971, for a "peaceful agreement" with Israel, which stunned the West, did not in fact represent a material change in policy, Haikal explained on February 26. As Sadat said on February 28, before the National Council of Palestine: "The liberation of the territories is what we have chosen *for this stage.* Revolutionary Arab thought must define the stages of a consistent and diligent policy out of the necessity that all the various strategies used in the confrontation with the enemy should flow out of one grand strategy. This will assure the victory of the Arab will."

The use of the term "peace" in the Arab context is another example of the earlier cited fallacy of equivalents in the two civilizations. The fact that Arabs do not think of war and peace in either/or fashion, as Westerners do, and indeed regard protracted warfare as normal, is mirrored in their multiple and flexible conceptions of "peace." The term they have used in connection with the American "peace initiative" is *salaam,* meaning less than real peace, and is more closely equivalent to our notion of an armistice. *Sulh,* or real peace, has been emphatically ruled out by the Arabs and is not used to refer to the present diplomatic activity.

Soon after the October War (December 7, 1973), the editor-in-chief of Egypt's leading weekly magazine, *Al-Mussawar,* spelled out the difference unmistakably:

"The English word 'peace' can be translated into Arabic as both *sulh* and *salaam,* whereas in Arabic, there is a difference between the two. *Sulh* is one thing, *salaam* another.

"The conference that everyone is talking about, the one to be held in Geneva to solve the problems of the Middle East, is liable to confuse these two words because of their single meaning in the European languages, and as a result, the meaning of the conference might not be clear to others."

The article goes on to explain that Israel can have *salaam* in exchange for a total acceptance of present Arab demands.

"But *sulh* is another thing altogether. *Sulh* means that the Jews of Palestine—and I repeat and emphasize the expression, Jews of Palestine—will return to their senses and will dwell under one roof and under one flag with the Arabs of Palestine, in a secular state devoid of any bigotry or racialism, proportional to their respective numerical ratio in 1948.

"By this I mean that the original Palestinian Jews and their children and grandchildren shall remain on the Palestinian soil and will live there with the original Palestinian Arabs. The Jews who came from abroad will return to their countries of origin, where they lived as did their fathers and forefathers before 1948—for these countries bear them no ill will."

Having ignored the strategy of phases our press could hardly fail to announce utopia upon hearing "peace," whose meaning it equally ignores. To grasp the magnitude of this achievement, in view of its heavy coverage of an area in which these things are openly and frequently discussed, one would have to compare it with foreign reporting from Washington, in the last two years, of a kind that managed not to take cognizance of Watergate, or only obliquely so. It is all the more unlikely that the people of America understand the emotive, symbolic content and rationale of Arab strategy. The fact is that settlement of the traumatic defeat of 1967 had itself assumed the nature of a test of the Arab cause. Observers in the West are well aware of the Arabs' insistence on complete or virtually complete restoration of territorial losses, and also tend to believe that Israel cannot have peace without this. But in the Arab context, the "liquidation of the traces of aggression" (as they invariably call withdrawal) is actually conceived as a test of the Arab ability to bring about Israel's demise, not as a touchstone for peaceful coexistence. Acquiescence in Jewish statehood on moral grounds is out of the question, which means that Israel's only hope lies in her military power; if that power can be mullified or made irrelevant, Jewish statehood is doomed.

The elaboration of this article of faith is best left to Haikal —not merely because of his articulateness, but because in the following passage he is captured in a moment of quiet, reflective conversation with another Arab intellectual, and hence cannot be faulted for vain posturing:

very interesty

"Abdul Nasser [Haikal recalls] could not hope for a positive response from Israel [to the Rogers initiative of June 1970], for he knew that Israel would never accept total withdrawal. I believe that Abdul Nasser viewed the issue of withdrawal as the testing ground which would transform the issue into being purely one of territory. Would Israel withdraw from all the occupied territories or would it refuse to do so? That was the crucial question; he regarded everything else as secondary at that stage.

"Abdul Nasser was certain, nevertheless, that Israel would not accept total withdrawal, otherwise everything it had hoped to gain through what it did in 1967 would be lost, all the objectives of the campaign would remain unrealized."

The interviewer asks: "Could you elaborate a little more on this? Are you saying that, if Israel were to withdraw, all its objectives would remain unrealized?" and Haikal answers: "Right. Why did Israel carry out the 1967 aggression? For two obvious reasons: in the first place, to prove that it has the upper hand as far as military strength is concerned—for military strength is the trump card; secondly, to acquire new territory and at the same time to undermine Arab claims to formerly occupied territories. . . .

"Once again, total Israeli withdrawal, if it were to take place, would be tantamount to showing that military strength is irrelevant to the outcome of the conflict, that the military factor is not decisive in the Middle East conflict, that it is perhaps capable of producing spectacular tactical results, but that these results will be shortlived.

". . . If you could succeed in bringing it about, you would have passed sentence on the entire state of Israel. . . ."[7]

It should be clear from this that what in the West's imagination of the events of October may appear as a bolstering of Arab self-esteem required for facing up to the Jewish state, would be in the authentic Arab context precisely the reason why one need not do it. Which is why "October" signifies in the Arab world the beginning of the end of Zionism, as Sadat himself has repeatedly affirmed.[8] The idea that it means the start of conciliation with it would strike Arabs as preposterous and abusive.

Even more disturbing perhaps is the continuation in the Arab world, including Egypt, of anti-Jewish agitation of both the traditional Muslim and the modern European kinds. It is idle to dwell on the fact that the several Arabic editions of the hoax *The Protocols of the Elders of Zion*, of Adolf Hitler's *Mein Kampf* and other notorious anti-Jewish tracts have not been removed from bookstores or libraries, since new ones are appearing alongside the old. Two anti-semitic tracts were included in the packages presented to each journalist accompanying French Foreign Minister Jobert in January of 1974 as the gift of King Faisal. Anti-semitic items appear randomly in the Arab press. Beirut's *Al-Bairak*, in a report from Damascus on June 26, 1974, described a meeting there between Lebanese politicians and Syrian leaders, including President Assad, Foreign Minister Haddam and ranking Baath party officials. To a Syrian suggestion that "the Arabs remember Hitler favorably," a Lebanese guest replied that "he would have saved us from the Zionists," urging that Nazism not be condemned and suggesting that the number of Jews killed by Nazis was greatly exaggerated, since "enormously large groups" had managed to escape extermination. (Sadat himself, as already mentioned, once published a eulogy for the Führer in an Egyptian journal.)

The struggle with Israel is, in the popular mind, the lingering struggle with a people demeaned and damned for all times, even since the days of the Prophet. A pamphlet distributed to Egyptian troops in the October War calls on them to kill the vicious outcasts of humankind everywhere. In Damascus the Baath leaders may cite more contemporary arguments against the foe, but their tanks on the Golan front bore the injunction "Death to the Infidels," and officers explained their purpose as punishment for a contemptible subject people presuming to be rulers.[9]

Even the sophisticated Arab leaders still betray a startling mentality in this connection. The old conviction that the Jews run the world is not dead; they are invariably "discovered" behind any untoward development. On May 10, 1974, the chief editor of the Cairo weekly *Akhbar al-Yom*, Ihsan Abd al-Quddous, a confidant of Sadat, explained that Israel was behind the Watergate affair, the security scandal in West Germany which led to the resignation of Chancellor Brandt, as well as the defeat of the Gaullists in the French presidential campaign. The view that the Jews engineered Nixon's downfall, as punishment for his late turn toward the Arabs, is widespread in the Arab world. Ahmed Zaki al-Yamani, the Saudi Minister whom some Americans regard as the epitome of a new, rational Arab man, explained to a group of American notables in New York that the continued embargo on oil shipments to the Netherlands was to punish the Dutch for sending their troops to fight the Arabs in the October War, a stunned participant related to this writer. An assertion that American troops also fought them in the last war was made by a high Egyptian officer in talking with American visitors more recently.[10]

Especially disturbing is a tendency to dispute the humanity of Israeli Jews. Anis Mansour, an editor of *Akhbar al-Yom*, has published a book on the native Israeli Jews, the so-called sabra generation, which he discussed in late December of 1973 on Radio Cairo. He described the sabra as "an odd type of human being, who reminds us of the story of Frankenstein, that monster of the horror films from the beginnings of the cinema, a form of creature created by some factory. . . . This type of 'manufactured' creature from the kibbutzim is a form of wild animal, a fundamentally hardened generation void of all human emotion. For this reason he has no spiritual depth, is absent of humanity, has no brother, father or mother. . . ."[11]

part six
The Evolving Middle East

11. Do the Arabs Want Peace?

In the Arab consciousness the meaning of "October" is an epochal triumph of momentous proportions, a turning of the tide of history against the West and its Zionist implant in the Arab homeland. While Westerners understand that American intervention in the war merely avoided yet another humiliating defeat for the Arabs, *they* understand that they not only dealt Israel a severe blow, but have broken the back of the foe, militarily as well as politically, once and for all. If past foreign salvaging operations left Arabs feeling that they had not been defeated—as after the 1956 war—the last version convinced them that they had indeed defeated Israel on the field of battle. Among the achievements of Egypt's attack in October are cited the following: 1) Israel's military defeat has changed the map of the Middle East; 2) Israel suffered its defeat from "secure borders"; 3) Egypt proved the falseness of Israel's security doctrine; 4) Israel's concept of air supremacy has lost its validity; and more.[1] Confidence has grown in the Arab world that every successive war will prove increasingly more disastrous for Israel.

Never having enjoyed a sense of legitimacy among Arabs, the Jewish state lost also its deterrence standing. Arabs see the Israelis as vincible, as easily overwhelmable, flashy but unsubstantial militarily. Their past successes were just flukes generated by trickery, gimmicks and the power of the gentiles.

"October" has revealed them for what they really are, a "paper tiger," as Colonel Qadhafi put it to a Lebanese journal recently, on August 11, 1974. Just before October, the Libyan had warned the Arabs that attacking Israel with regular armies would prove suicidal. In the frequent threats of new war, should Israel fail to submit soon to Arab demands, there was a new ring. Before October, they were frankly intended to "spark" international diplomacy for pressure on Israel; since the war, they were intended for Israel as well, a direct threat, a real military option.

The new military confidence and the vast new treasures of the oil-producing countries spurred ambitious plans for the establishment of Arab arms industries. The American promise of a nuclear reactor to Egypt generated excitement around the idea of atomic armament for the Arabs. Foreign Minister Fahmi of Egypt repeatedly stated that, should it become known that Israel was producing nuclear devices, Egypt and other Arab countries would also exercise the atomic option. A few days after the last Fahmi statement, on June 22, 1974, President Sadat said he believed Israel very probably already had exercised the atomic option. Those who remembered Fahmi's statement would understand the frightful implication. In case they did not, the Egyptian delegate at the Islamic Conference at Kuala Lumpur raised the point again two days later. A remark by the Saudi Defense Minister may have indicated that his country was ready to shoulder the principal financial burden of Egypt's nuclear development. In an editorial published on June 24, 1974, Cairo's *Al-Ahram* warned Israel that the only alternative to the Arab idea of a settlement was a more destructive war than all the previous ones, one that might assume nuclear dimensions.

In Arab eyes, without the reason for being, there remained for Israel only to accommodate to modalities of advancing nothingness. The belief persisted among Arabs, even in previous periods, that Israel was artificial, factitious, a merely temporary aberration. Now they are vindicated and have presented various events in Israel and abroad as further proof. The Israeli political crisis following the war was explained on Radio Cairo as indicating that Israel has none of the prerequisites of a state;[2] the economic woes were interpreted in the same light, as was any news of social strain. In view of the certainty about where matters were heading, the Arabs' reaction to Israeli statements of policy, looking forward to substantive negotiations on new borders and normal diplomatic and economic intercourse, was one of disbelief bordering on genuine amusement and sometimes merely sadness at the crazed and incorrigible nature of the Zionists. Hence the puzzling requirement for "good behavior" from Israel on which the Egyptian offer of nonbelligerency against acceptance of all Arab demands was conditioned.

An essential part of the heightened confidence in Israel's demise derived from a perceived shift in America's position under Kissinger's stewardship, since that state's existence without the latter's constant support was deemed unthinkable. Typical of a public-relations-minded version of the faith was this explanation by Egypt's Minister of Information to American visitors of his country's offer of peace while rejecting Zionism: "Yes, Israel is a Zionist state today. But we will persuade America to stop supporting Israel. Israel is totally dependent on U.S. support. Once this support is withdrawn, the state will be weakened. Then there are many divisions inside Israel—between Ashkenazi and Sephardi and so on. The Zionist state will fall of its own weaknesses. If Israel remains a Zionist state, that remains to be seen. Who would have believed that Israel would have given up one piece of territory? We differ in history and perception. It is not static, flat or predictable. Israeli policy has been based on establishing 'new facts' to acquire new acquisitions. The war of 1973 created new facts in favor of the Arabs. It achieved a basic change in the position of the U.S. and of many Israelis. Therefore one cannot predict that Israel will always remain Zionist in the classical, impractical way. No peace can be permanent unless this sort of irritation can be removed. . . ."[3]

Or, an Egyptian delegate, telling a United Nations body in New York on August 19, 1974, that the existence of Israel was an extravagant frivolity: "October came to wipe out the

June syndrome. Since October, Israel has lost its sex appeal and cancer in the area has turned into septic focus which will eventually be removed. The spoiled child of the Middle East has become the sick man of the Middle East. Minister Sapir himself said 'October cost us more than 7 billion. We cannot afford to fight such a war every couple of years; maybe the Arabs could.' In fact there would have been no longer an all Israeli state but for the huge American airlift and one wonders what kind of state is this as your political fallacy that needs blood transfusions in order to stay alive. Will it stay alive, as *The Sunday Times* once put the question, to see the year 2000? Israel, using business language, claims that it was a good American investment. October proved that it was a very bad investment. It did threaten to cut the veins that carry life to the world world, while Israel proved to be a paper tiger unable to defend its own very existence and while it appeared to be just a political luxury that the world could do without."

But the world was not yet prepared to let the Arabs *totally* defeat Israel, as Sadat put it to the Central Committee of the Arab Socialist Union on July 23, 1974, the anniversary of King Farouk's ouster. That task falls to the future. Meanwhile, he said the "good cards" in the Arabs' hands are continually increasing, not becoming fewer. Like other "moderates," he sought the steady erosion of whatever support for the foe lingered abroad, essentially in America. And there was a growing inclination to start tackling the very core, by engaging in "dialogue" elements of America's Jewish community. The message was invariably couched in positive, peaceful terms and urged return to fraternal coexistence, as in the good old days, the necessary divestment of Jewish statehood not being made too explicit. To "militants," seeking liquidation in one fell swoop, "moderates" answered that nothing they did really closed that option either, when appropriate.

Westerners who know the slender military basis of the Arabs' exultation may have wished to explain all that talk away as compensation for the impotence before the Israeli outrage. At a time when many Jews abroad shared the Arabs' voiced expectations as their own private and even public night-mares, the presumption surely was that they also were capable of discerning the same ominous signs. But the sanguineness of the Arabs' mood had to be witnessed to be believed.

The apparent success of Egypt's strategy of phases placed the *fedayeen* between jeopardy and opportunity. The Arabs' rising despair before the October War as to the chances ever to see recovery of any lost land was precipitously replaced by confidence in speedy and full return. Arabs believed and pub-licly averred that they had America's solemn pledge, through Kissinger, to this end. Soon after signing the troop disengage-ment pact, Egypt restated its continued adherence to the strat-egy by way of its Foreign Minister to the *fedayeen* and Youth Minister to the press in Beirut.[4] Now that full Israeli with-drawal was, as Sadat put it often, "a fact," he prodded the *fedayeen* to address the next phase, in the same manner.

The debate raging among the *fedayeen* and throughout the Arab world since the October War has been ignored in the West in much the same way as the earlier Egyptian debate on strategy was ignored. Like it, the more recent one was open and candid, and when concluded, its decision, like the previous one, was misunderstood in the West. Arguing for adoption of the strategy, a large majority of *fedayeen* leaders indicated that failure to do so would leave the Jordanians in control of the parts of Palestine from which Israel would be forced to with-draw at the Geneva conference. Since they were certain to use force to liquidate the *fedayeen* in those areas, as they had done in the past, it was imperative to come to Geneva and make Israel hand the areas over to the *fedayeen* themselves.

A strategy of phases was endorsed also as a particularly wise and efficient revolutionary strategy for the overthrow of the Jewish state itself. No achievement, however small, should be turned down, if it involved the weakening of the foe and the strengthening of the revolutionaries' position. The first stage would be the establishment of a "national authority" in every area from which Israel would retreat, no commitment being given and no circumstances allowed that would inhibit the struggle toward the final objective. This insistence was an explicit rejection of the notion of a "state"—as the *fedayeen* aim was invariably misconceived and misreported in the West—so as not to prejudice the struggle even semantically. "State" is reserved for the ultimate goal in all Palestine cleansed of Jewish dominion.

That the Arabs may be compelled to declare nonbelligerency in return for total Israeli withdrawal should not unduly alarm the *fedayeen*, argued the majority in their midst. For the continued struggle would not be determined by pieces of paper so much as by the resultant realities. The blow to Israel's status and morale entailed in a forced withdrawal all the way back to the 1967 lines would be such as to shake the state's very foundations. Israel's image of success would be shattered, immigration would fall, the economy would stagnate. Even the limited setbacks since October 6 had some of these effects on Israel. Hence Israel may resist pressure for total withdrawal with desperate resolution, thus taking the onus for the failure to make peace and leaving the *fedayeen* in a greatly enhanced position in the West. Even if Israel did withdraw to the 1967 lines, the Arabs would still be able to demand that the 1947 United Nations Palestine Partition Resolution be implemented, requiring further withdrawal to a virtually untenable territorial shape, to be filled moreover with masses of Arab refugees, also according to United Nations resolutions. A host of other options was cited, among them a demand for the cessation of all Jewish immigration to Israel, presumably in order to assure the security of neighboring Arab countries, which even a much contracted Israel was certain to reject, further justifying continued struggle against it.

A minority warned against entrapment during the negotiating process into unintended concessions, stressing the difficulties for any Palestinian entity sandwiched between Israel and Jordan, and claiming that the successes of the regular Arab armies in October did not render less valid the *fedayeen* earlier determination to develop the struggle against Israel into a protracted people's war on the Vietnam model; and urged defiance of the Arab states that pushed them to Geneva. The minority expressed confidence that the masses would support the *fedayeen* in this even against their own rulers.

In adopting the explicit termed "phased political program," in June of 1974, the Palestine National Council stressed the purely tactical nature of achieving a foothold in Palestine toward the liquidation of Jewish dominion in its entirety. The anxious determination to eschew ensnarement is expressed in virtually every sentence of the text. While *fedayeen* leaders occasionally indulged the Western journalists' insistence on speaking of a "state" instead of the proper "national authority," they were remarkably frank in talking to foreigners. But they were usually translated or explained away in reports abroad. In *The New York Times* the *fedayeen* demand was almost invariably presented as terminal for only parts of Palestine, and even official Arab statements were amended to read in this wise, while quotation marks were handled so as to suggest authenticity for the false translation.[5] On the rare occasions when the original phrases were mentioned, they were discounted in the report. "But there is no doubt," read one explanation, "that for the Palestinians negotiation would mean accepting the permanent existence of Israel."[6] Anticipating some provocative statements in Arafat's address to the United Nations, a report from Cairo suggested that this would merely be demagogic.[7] When *fedayeen* statements were couched in code words largely unfamiliar to foreign readers, there was no indication of their meaning in the original context.[8]

The appearance of the *fedayeen* at the United Nations General Assembly provided an interesting case study of the discounting process. Both in his address and in their meetings with journalists and others, Arafat and his aides not merely held rigidly to their stated position in the usual form, but carefully avoided any indication of weakness behind it, heaping contempt on any reference by others to the Jewish state. *The New York Times* report of Arafat's address (November 14, 1974) carried headlines suggesting that his intent toward the foe was moot, as if destruction of the state was not a necessary prerequisite of his objective but just a partisan interpretation of it. Comment in the newspaper and elsewhere almost invariably addressed this as a moot question, either interpretation being equally likely and cogent. The television networks, main source of news for most Americans, presented Arafat's address without indicating the partisan interpretation, with one exception, the featured commentary on one network's broadcast actually treating the *fedayeen* stance as if negotiable.

The egregious bluntness and contemptuous manner could not fail to disturb many, among them diplomats and journalists (editorial comment in the above issue of *The Times* was at odds with its front page, terming Arafat's goal unequivocally opposed to Israel's existence). But the process of erosion was already setting in, as the normal interposition of interpreters of Arab intent was again increasingly displacing the original actors. Laymen find it difficult to trust their spontaneous impressions under challenge by "experts." Thus diplomats on the spot, and even Arab sources, were soon after reported to have discounted Arafat's words as mere rhetoric. The readers of *The Times* were immediately informed by its man in Cairo that an unnamed Egyptian had told him that Arafat had to say these things or risk credibility among his rank and file, particularly on his first appearance in a world forum—and besides, "while Mr. Arafat did not declare his acceptance of the state of Israel, neither did he say anything that would commit him against accepting it at a later stage."[9] The educational network summoned the expertise of *Newsweek*'s senior man in the Middle East, Arnaud de Borchgrave, who discounted Arafat's words in a similar manner;[10] the *Time* magazine authority, brought to a special program on the day of the address, also discounted the "rhetoric."

Illustrating the tendency of Westerners to press hopeful construction upon blunt antagonism was the comment by Senator Frank Moss, Democrat of Utah, following an informal meeting of a group of American legislators with members of the P.L.O. at the United Nations. The latter were relentlessly obdurate in their position, resorting to the usual sarcasm in responding to their interlocutors' reference to Israel. But "Senator Moss said he had gained an impression from the 'very articulate' Palestinians that they were ready for a compromise on their proclaimed goals of struggle until the defeat of Israel."[11]

Fedayeen appear generally more cautious with American audiences than with other foreigners. Naif Hawatmeh, in reply to a German journalist's question whether the goal would still be the liquidation of Israel after a Palestinian state was established in the West Bank and the Gaza Strip, said (*Deutsche Zeitung*, April 19, 1974): "Yes. We shall not relent on this goal because our purpose is the establishment of a democratic state in all of Palestine. A state in the occupied territories is not an obstacle, it is a starting point." In his interview with Juan de Onis (*The Times*, May 21, 1974), Hawatmeh used much less explicit language for the same purpose.

The likelihood of an American popular medium of information presenting the expressions of Arab consciousness among Arabs is nearly nil. For instance, Arafat sharing his thoughts with militants in Jedda, Saudi Arabia (on February 24, 1974, as cited by The Voice of Palestine broadcasting from North Yemen): "We are now in the tenth year of our Revolution, which is the longest of Arab revolutions. The Algerian one lasted seven and a half years while that of the Palestinians had its beginnings in 1917. . . . The Ramadan War (of October 1973) was an important turning point. . . . For the first time the decision to fight was an Arab decision and its most important result was this war. Perhaps in ten years' time another decision will be taken to liquidate the arrogant enemy completely. . . . The decisive word will be spoken by Arab solidarity and Arab weapons. We have always said that it is not easy and that the war is a long, drawn-out one. We did not say that we would eat lunch in Jedda and dinner in Tel Aviv. We did not lie. We were asked: 'Why did you train the Young Lions [*fedayeen* children corps]?' We replied: 'It is this generation which will reach the sea.' "[12]

But it must be conceded that few Westerners possess the training necessary to understand Arabs in their own terms. One finds them among the academic Orientalists, who are not to be confused with diplomatic "Arabists" and political scientists and international affairs specialists writing on the Middle East. Even when not simply dismissing offensive or puzzling Arab messages out of hand as meaningless, since Arabs presumably do not mean what they say—a mark of expertise—the usual understanding occurs in Western terms that are often not equivalent to counterparts in the original, which involve radically different concepts of time, war, peace, world order, conscience, morality and other weighty notions. Since many Arab statements make little sense in the Western mentality, they lose credibility as absurd. For instance, the idea of a protracted peace campaign as war seems strange in the West, but fits well with the pertinent concepts in the Arab setting. The tendency to translate Arabs in terms of Western experience and mentality forever produces "moderates" such as Arabs themselves never knew and "acceptance" of the Jewish state where the very idea is nauseating, and so on. Western diplomats view Arabs running from the field of battle to fight another day and deduce that they do not really have their heart in the cause; or Arabs emerge in near paroxysm of exultation from another war, and the diplomats suppose that they are battle-weary enough to desire peace. (American policy in the region is in fact premised on this judgment.)

An expression of the Arabs' sense of ascendancy since the October War has been the toughening of their posture in the indirect bargaining carried on by Kissinger since the war. There was a quick build-up of the international status of the *fedayeen,* culminating in the unprecedented invitation to them by the United Nations General Assembly to address it as exclusive representatives of the Palestinians, immediately followed by the formal endorsement of this position by the Arab summit at Rabat, on October 28, 1974, forcing the removal of Hussein's Jordan from further dealings. By this coup the Arabs transcended the internationally accepted framework for a settlement since the June War, based on the vaunted Resolution 242, staking out by fiat a more extreme position for Israel and the United States on a take-or-leave basis. The new framework put the question of Jewish statehood itself formally on the agenda of the international community. An interesting comment on the nature of Kissinger's policy is the fact that the Arab forces, on which its success was predicated, had themselves endorsed the extremist Rabat resolution or the P.L.O. that dealt a setback to the policy. Israeli leaders complained that Kissinger had assured them that Sadat and Faisal would prevent this development, when they proved to have done nothing to thwart its emergence.[13]

The Arabs seemed utterly certain that they would impose their will on both the United States and Israel. That the latter would resist as if its life were at stake was taken for granted, since Arabs understand, as Israelis do, negotiation with the *fedayeen* to mean negotiating one's disappearance. Hence Israel must be forced into this by irresistible circumstances, abandonment by America being the essential condition. That they would sooner or later make America acquiesce seemed certain to the Arab rulers. (A hint of weakness in American support for Israel came on the heels of the Rabat decision, as President Ford in an impromptu news conference indicated that he wanted Israel to talk for peace to anyone, the Jordanians or the *fedayeen*. The spontaneous remark was quickly followed by assurances by State Department spokesmen that American policy had not changed. But word was leaked also that talk of such change was merely "premature," for sooner or later even Israel would have to adjust to the new situation. Ford's subsequent statement "indicated that he did not want to be pinned down on United States views about the Palestine Liberation Organization.")[14] There were threats of a new oil embargo, should America not soon accept the Arab posture. King Hassan of Morocco indicated that the Arabs would prevail even without one, since oil prices were emasculating the West financially at a fast rate: " 'The United States, because of its economic difficulties and inflation, will no longer be able to go on bailing out Israel financially,' he said."[15]

Rabat marks for the Arabs a historic turning point in that they believe the world is finally ready to start getting used to the idea of Israel's eventual non-being. They were not prepared to compromise on their draft resolution before the United Nations General Assembly at the conclusion of the debate on Palestine soon after, if compromise meant even an obscure reference to Israel in the text of the resolution, which is what the Common Market countries wanted. They settled for a smaller majority behind their original text and were obviously not dismayed when some foreign sources noted the poignant absence of any mention of Israel in a majority's summation of such a debate in the international forum. That this was part of a pattern was indicated somewhat earlier at the UNESCO conference in Paris, where another anti-Israeli resolution was publicly explained to mark the foe's nothingness as an international datum. It was the delegate from Lebanon, the member of the Arab League deemed least hostile to Israel, who declared that the vote to exclude that country from its European regional group meant that "Israel belongs nowhere."[16] (It was called the "spiritual abolition of Israel," by a group of French writers, artists and scientists who denounced the step.)[17] In future diplomatic dealings, since Arabs view the P. L. O. achievement as irreversible, they might even consent to substitute Jordan as receiver of occupied Palestinian territory as a tactic to speed further Israeli retreats.

12. How Much Will Israel Yield?

Israel emerged from the October War in a state of shock. The people's gloom and dejection were unmistakable. The Israelis spoke of the "earthquake" that had hit them and reports abroad abounded, describing their condition as troubled, sad and insecure, even on the first anniversary of the war. But the reasons for this gloom were not unmistakable when viewed by outsiders. Their inclination was to overstate the Arab role by citing upsetting improvements in military performance and the grave casualties it claimed. In fact, Israelis now think better of Arab armies than before the war, but still do not doubt their own overwhelming superiority; as for the losses, they were painful for the small, compact country, but this had not before plunged it into dejection. Israelis emerged from their first major war, in 1949, with almost ten times as many casualties in proportion to their numbers, yet their mood was jubilant. In reality, the shock had set in before the full extent of the losses was known; when it was realized, it only deepened the gloom.

The roots of Israel's dejection obviously go deeper. Some foreign observers have sensed this, but their probing barely touches the raw nerve in Israel's profound travail. They are right in citing the great dependence on American weapons, money and political support, but the Israelis' trouble transcends their fear that the leverage will be employed to force them into

painful concessions. It is in fact a shattering glimpse of the
cosmic tragedy of Jewishness.

For Israelis themselves there is little doubt about when the
shock came. "I think the traumatic experience of the Israelis
was not the sudden unexpected attack on October 6," said the
Israeli novelist Amos Oz, "but the Russian-American ultimatum
on October 22. Namely, you are not allowed to win this war.
You are not allowed to win any war any more. This war, this
game, is over. We can help you not to be defeated, but you are
not allowed to end the war and defeat the enemy."[1] Other
Israelis use similar words often when pinpointing the shock.
According to the university professor Shalom Abarbanel, "a
'mood of depression' set in when the people realized that neither
Washington nor Moscow would ever allow Israel to achieve a
decisive victory over the Arab states."[2] Interviews with many
others confirm this observation.

Modern Zionism was above all else a rebellion against
Jewish history, a valiant and desperate attempt at "normaliz-
ing" the Jewish people, to be at last like other peoples, to control its own fate. The achievement of statehood gave the Jews
power over their affairs in one country and even abroad in
many cases. As a small state with few resources, Israel was
heavily dependent on other powers, but even the successful
pleading in olden days with rulers of Jewish communities in the
diaspora could not be compared with sovereign power, even
of a little nation. Though they had to bow to foreign pressure
on many occasions—like other powers—the feeling of being
ultimately in charge of their destiny was unimpaired. They
would be grateful to a great power's disposition to supply them
with vital weapons, but would insist on specifying the par-
ticulars; and sever their dependence on others at the earliest
possible date. The insistence on retaining control even in weakness and dependence asserted itself with truculence at the beginning of the first substantial Jewish military force as a function of British requirements in World War Two. The last word
in all matters in the incipient *Palmach* units, formally in the
framework of the British army, was by Jewish authority. The

fiercely independent streak of Israelis was well known to American officials who dealt with them, though the popular imagination had all along the notion that the Jewish state was governed in Washington.

The aftermath of the June War marked unprecedented assertiveness, even with the great powers. Anxiously at first, but with increasing confidence, Israel resisted American pressure to relinquish tangible gains for dubious promises, and the tougher Israel became the less sanguine were the American officials in pursuit of retreats. Within a few years after the war, Israelis were beginning to feel that they had indeed reached the point where even the great powers were acknowledging failure to move them. The October War suddenly allowed the powers to restore their sway with a vengeance and Israel would not be permitted to punish its tormentors; it would be told to spare them and even to succor the trapped aggressors and it would obey. There rose, said Oz, "the haunting fear that Israelis are once again Jews with no control over their own fate."

And the nightmare is that they are "Jews" again in a world gone berserk against them, nations vying with other nations in manifestations of antagonism. While Russians, Koreans, Vietnamese (and even Japanese for the *fedayeen*) add themselves to the overwhelming masses of Arabs already engaged in battle against a small people, others deny Israeli's their airspace or their ports. Their attackers are cheered in various capitals; the slayers of their women and children are invited into the halls of the United Nations as honored guests, where their call for the liquidation of the Jews' state elicits a standing ovation. The taste of pogrom was back in Israeli mouths.

Kissinger had injured Israel at the roots. It is difficult to overstate the importance for Israel's functioning of the sense of the ability to best and confound tormentors. If Jewish blood can be shed with impunity, the whole historic enterprise has been for naught, no matter what else was achieved. The manner in which wars with Arabs were concluded greatly influenced the climate of the subsequent period in the country's life and work. The War of Independence was followed by exulting boom in virtually all fields of endeavor; the diplomatic defeat in the wake of the military success in 1956 was followed, after brief excitement, by pessimism and declining numbers of immigrants. The exhilarating outcome of the June War initiated a period of enormous growth. Israel's success greatly attracted immigrants and funds from abroad, both as gifts and investments, stimulated its own people in virtually every area of work and emboldened even the Jewry of the Soviet Union to open defiance of the regime in support of Zionism.

Israel emerged from the October War not as a success, despite the most impressive military performance ever. Depression set in in virtually every area from mental health to the economy. There was an immediate rise of ten percent in the number of Israelis seeking treatment in the country's community mental health centers.[3] Instead of the normal 7 or 8 percent increase in the Gross National Product, there was actually a drop in the months after the war. There was also a sharp drop in immigration; while the annual rate for 1973 before October ran to over 50,000, it fell to only over 20,000 for the balance of the year, and to under 20,000 for the first half of 1974.[4] The rate of immigration had always been tightly linked to the rate of economic growth; an unsuccessful Israel does not strongly pull Jews to its shores, even as tourists (of whom the rate fell also). The number of Israelis said to be contemplating emigration rose sharply after the war. There was a marked privatism and self-indulgence among them throughout a period punctuated by warnings of impending war. Less than half the number needed for a civil guard to combat terrorism volunteered for service, even in the wake of bomb attacks.[5] The stringent measures to save the economy triggered labor unrest and riots in November of 1974.

But in the crucial attitudes on war and peace, on territorial concessions and Arab intent, little, if any, change occurred. Assumptions to the contrary disregarded their deep-rootedness, for they had been long evolving, in some respects long before the June War, growing firmer in its aftermath and, in some ways, as a result of the experience of the October War as well.

The misreading of Israeli attitudes has merely repeated the error in the widespread optimism accompanying the first initiatives of the Nixon Administration in the Middle East soon after the June War. Nearly four years into the post-bellum period, *Time* commissioned a Louis Harris poll in Israel, and discovered the startling fact that Jerusalem's "tough and hypercautious" diplomatic posture indeed reflected overwhelming genuine sentiment in that country. "If any U.S., Soviet or Arab policymakers," it stated, "assume that there is a significant dove faction in Israel, they appear sorely mistaken."[6] The American policymakers who were so long in error on this matter are essentially the same ones who continued to direct United States affairs in the Middle East afterward.

The nature of Israeli attitudes need not have been a mystery abroad, since reliable domestic opinion polls were taken in the country frequently. Many Americans are exposed to what may appear a fair sample of Israeli opinion, while in effect it vastly over-represents a fringe faction in the population. Thus ironically those whom one would usually describe as "informed" constituted the core of the misguided. The "dovish" faction in Israel happens to be disproportionately strong among people who are extremely articulate and particularly likely to speak to Americans, both in Israel and abroad; academics, artists and journalists maintain fairly close contact with their American colleagues and tend also to accept their views on matters concerning Israel. As a result, these Americans may mistake congenial views as representative. Indeed, because their really appreciative audiences are in the States, rather than at home, the Israeli dissenters tend to come to America, thus furthering such false impressions. There is something of a career to be made as a "reasonable" or "even-handed" Israeli in the American arena, a role that Amos Elon appears to have garnered in recent years. (For the Arab counterpart we now have Sana Hassan, and together or singly they are very much in demand in publishing and on the speaking circuit, their participation in televised discussions of Middle East problems being *de rigueur*. Since Jewish organizations are heavy consumers of this kind of output, ignorance is also widespread in the American Jewish community.

Systematic surveys revealed that Israelis after the June-War rejected in overwhelming numbers the total or near total withdrawal to the 1967 lines demanded by Arabs and endorsed by American proposals for settlement, even when asked to consider heavy American pressure. Many felt that the Arabs were not yet ready for real peace but insisted that Israel reply affirmatively to every Arab initiative for direct or indirect negotiations. The territories which official Jerusalem indicated were not really negotiable—East Jerusalem, the Golan Heights and Sharm el Sheikh—were also those which nearly all respondents insisted on keeping. Readiness to return parts of the Sinai, of the West Bank and the Gaza Strip was markedly more pronounced. The widespread assumption in the United States, that younger Israelis were more "dovish" than their elders, was shown to be fallacious.

There was some sharp fluctuation of opinion during the October War and shortly afterward toward harder positions. When Israelis were canvassed later, the pre-war attitudes surfaced with only insubstantial changes. The Israel Institute of Applied Social Research found that 84% of Israelis were convinced that the Arabs still sought to destroy their state, their positions on territory not differing much either (thus the proportion of those favoring return of some areas to Egypt actually fell a little since the spring before the war), while 86% believed another war was possible, perhaps within a year.[7] A study of Israel's position on territories by Bernard Reich for the State Department concluded that the same considerations which had determined it before the October War were shaping it in the present.

What changed was the inclination of Israel's leaders to consider parting with portions of territory deemed not ultimately essential more readily than before. This was due to the worsened international position from that of October, both in the sense that Israel hoped to win sympathy abroad, especially in the United States, by appearing ready to take risks for peace;

and that pieces of territory could be traded for periods of non-belligerency—buying time with real estate, as some of them have put it. They hoped to test also the notion that the foe (especially Egypt) could be turned around toward new directions. The feeling in America that they engaged in this process because they were inclined to think that the foe had changed (presumably because of Kissinger's efforts) was erroneous.

Premier Rabin could not have spoken more plainly than when he replied to an interviewer's question after the conclusion of the troop disengagement pacts with Egypt and Syria: "As far as I know Egypt is willing to arrive at a settlement with Israel on the basis of a complete Israeli withdrawal to the lines of June 4, 1967, and the creation of a Palestinian State in Judaea, Samaria and the Gaza Strip. Now, if you ask me— won't such an arrangement bring peace and permit Israel's survival?—my answer is clearly no. If you ask me—isn't Egypt today prepared to arrive at a settlement with Israel, one which will give us peace and security?—my answer is again no."[8]

part seven
Kissinger's Lasting Impact

13. Russia, Influence and Oil

On the eve of Nixon's tour of the Middle East, hailed as the crowning of the epochal turn in the region and its relations with America, one journalist paused long enough to attach a rare, disturbing afterthought to the usual paeans to the architect of the grand success, Secretary Kissinger. Some Middle East specialists, wrote Bernard Gwertzman, dissented from the heady convictions abroad in the land, chiefly because they feared that the Secretary's interventions in the region had engendered excessively ambitious expectations among Arabs. After he had engineered some more Israeli withdrawals, a final deal will have to be struck, the Arabs expecting to get everything back, the Israelis insisting on keeping some of the occupied land. What happens then, they asked.

"The Administration hopes that through trips such as Mr. Nixon's and the continuing improvement in Arab-American relations, underscored by the agreement [on joint study groups in various fields] yesterday with Saudi Arabia, a crisis can be avoided. Mr. Kissinger and Mr. Nixon believe that the trend toward moderation by the Arabs can be accelerated so that when the time comes for a final settlement with Israel they will make some territorial compromise to bring about peace. If that happens, the American role will again be applauded and Mr. Nixon's visit remembered as a step along the road to a settle-

ment. But the experts warn that if in the final stages a settlement eludes the two sides, and fighting erupts again, the United
States might be held responsible and Mr. Nixon's trip remembered as part of a cruel hoax."[1]

The chickens were beginning to come home to roost much
sooner than anticipated. Within just two months the clouds of
yet another war were already clearly over the Middle East and
even the admiring press was getting glimpses of the persistent
"normality" of the region even after Kissinger's intervention.
"In the opinion of officials here and in Washington," reported
The Times man in Jerusalem, "most of the developments do not
augur well for peace. On the contrary, they tend to reinforce
the grim estimate—held at the highest level here—that a new
round of Middle East fighting is inevitable in the next six
months-to-a-year unless there is substantial political movement.

"This prognosis is based on two gloomy but realistic conclu-
sions:

"1. The October War, for all its bloodshed, did nothing to
alter or reduce the basic hostility between the Arab states and
Israel. Rather than encourage new, more conciliatory attitudes
on both sides, the 1973 fighting tended to reinforce the hard-
line positions. Israel's doubts about fundamental Arab intentions were strengthened, while the Arab pride and appetite for
more triumphs was whetted. Rather than opening the way to a
political settlement, the October fighting renewed the military
option as a feasible and potentially profitable alternative for the
Arab estates. Rather than reducing Israeli fears about the possibility of imminent attack, the war heightened them.

"2. None of the basic political issues that separate the two
sides—recognition, territory, Jerusalem and the future of the
Palestinians—were even partially resolved by the October War.
. . . In the months since the war, the two sides have been
basically jockeying for position. First they pushed for the best
arrangements they could make in the troop-separation agreements, sometimes arguing stubbornly over a few hundred yards
difference in the cease fire line. More recently, they have been
maneuvering in preparation for the next negotiating phase, and
simultaneously rebuilding their arsenals. . . ."[2]

By November, the world experienced the first full-scale war scare in the Middle East, about a year after a war had been fought. This fact alone is unprecedented even in the notoriously war-torn area. For while there were several wars before between Arabs and Israelis, there was always a period of grace between them, when, despite some posturing, more war was not immediately likely. Inter-war periods lasted between six and eleven years and were the sole experience of peace that Jews and Arabs could perhaps have hope of for at all. The Kissinger intervention in the October War now appeared to deny them even this miserable bit of quiet, since it demolished the pillars on which it could rest for several years between wars. The reason why relatively peaceful interludes of such duration obtained even among the fervent antagonists in the Middle East is that both sides had little incentive or interest in new war soon. Having crushed the Arabs on the battlefield, the Israelis could afford to enjoy their gains (even from the diplomatic fiasco after the 1956 war they rescued passage through the Straits of Tiran). Besides, the Arabs could not go to war, no matter how much they wished, for some years after a decisive defeat. As a consequence of Kissingerian "tilting" in the war and after, the post-October War period became the first in which previous restraints no longer obtained on either side. Not only were the Arabs theatening war almost without letup and with still credible armed force, but the idea of an Israeli preemptive strike was soon back in casual conversation.

The Secretary could see himself already in "mid-solution" for the record of the ages,[3] but from more mundane perspectives the Middle East he helped shape was clearly hysterical and more ominous than ever. Now the area was permanently agitated on the brink of disaster, the threat of war hanging over it and international diplomacy feverishly seeking to avert its outbreak, if only for a while. A war scare was scarcely allayed, with United Nations Secretary-General Waldheim rushing to the Middle East, seemingly just in the nick of time, just as the mandate of his buffer force on the Golan front was about to expire, in late November of 1974, and the Israelis already indicated they expected war to erupt in the spring. He himself warned that events in the next month could be critical for the region.[4]

What had been thought to be a confident and deliberate American policy for achieving peace in the area by stages appeared rather as improvisation, not in control of events so much as rolling with the punches. It was the Arabs who dictated the pace and the setting, on petroleum, at the United Nations, and in the region itself, and for the United States to draw the consequences and to accommodate, as they themselves bluntly told it every time, after Rabat, after getting Arafat to the United Nations, after each price hike or refusal to reduce the cost of oil. They counted on Secretary Kissinger to find ways out of the dilemmas they posed and to keep the momentum going despite the toughening of their stance. There was always room for another Israeli retreat, no matter what the troubles elsewhere, and Arab leaders invariably encouraged him to go ahead as he toured the region in the aftermath of Rabat. "We shall always be, in Egypt, ready to regain whatever land we can," said Sadat.[5] And American diplomacy was hard at work getting an Israeli retreat where it seemed alone possible at the moment, in the Sinai. One could not really know where one was going, but one knew one could not stand still; there had to be movement or there would be disaster. Between the devil and the deep sea one could always try for yet another Israeli retreat, and if that failed, one could always duck in anticipation of the holocaust to come. The power with potentially decisive influence on the fate of the Middle East had been relegated to fatalistic pandering to Arab leadership. He knows what we want, said an official of a small Arab state, Lebanon, of the Secretary of State of the superpower at the recent convening of the General Assembly in New York, and he is expected to deliver. Of course, the Arab stance had been no different before Kissinger, only now it was put to America with the confidence of command.

Control over events may be tested by the accuracy of prediction. The record of Kissingerian prediction of Middle Eastern events could hardly be worse. Washington was eagerly anticipating a lifting of the oil embargo to follow on the heels of the Egyptian troop disengagement pact, as Kissinger confidently indicated to associates and others, only to discover that the Arabs really wanted to keep the pressure on until after the Syrians got some satisfaction as well. His policy was equally expected for the same reason to bring the price of oil down, with even more disappointing results. Before Rabat the Secretary advised all and sundry of his confidence in Sadat and Faisal aborting the *fedayeen* resolution, only to have it pass unanimously. During the Egyptian disengagement talks with Kissinger, Sadat was widely reported to have given oral assurances that he would quickly rebuild the destroyed cities on the Suez Canal and reopen the waterway itself as a step to peace as quickly as technically feasible (the Israelis claiming additional promises to them through Kissinger on this score).[6] As soon as the waterway seemed nearly ready for navigation, the Egyptians reneged; now, said Foreign Minister Fahmi, "the Suez Canal will not be opened to world shipping until there had been a complete Israeli withdrawal east of the canal so as to make the waterway and the cities safe against Israeli surprise attack."[7] And it was the Egyptians who chided the Secretary for not having moved faster in the meantime.

The unprecedented denial of even a period of grace in the aftermath of Arab-Israeli war was ironically praised by State Department spokesmen as rare "balance"—for the first time at the end of any such war, offering the first real chance for peace. This was obviously a roundabout way of owning up to, and justifying, the "tilting" in the October War, but its real significance was in the light it threw on our policy makers' manner of thinking on the conflict as a whole. The conflict thus remained unresolved for so long *not* because the opposing claims may have been incompatible, but presumably because wars ended with one side too strong to make concessions and the other too humiliated to attempt any. The fact that this kind of outcome actually tended to resolve ordinary, compromisable conflicts, rather than the other way around, seemed not to occur to them. For where the issue was indeed just territorial, and not the very existence of antagonists, decisive wars ended in settlement. One need but glance at the border changes in the aftermath of World War Two in Asia and all over Europe. But the greater irony was that the military disparity of the past was precisely what maintained even a hint of balance between the Arabs and Israelis. For the only thing that the latter had to match the enormous disparity in numbers, resources and alliances favoring the Arabs was military ascendancy. To remove *it* for the sake of "balance," meant throwing the advantage to the Arabs completely, in effect unbalancing the Middle East, which explained better why it seemed in permanent crisis since the October War.

Since the diplomats' conception of things Middle Eastern had long been widely shared by the press and international affairs generalists, there was still a marked tendency to separate Kissinger's policy from its failures. Hence a strain to discount the latter as irrelevant to the validity of the former, or sheer bad luck. Thus *The Times* editorially termed the *fedayeen* triumph at the United Nations no less than "Invitation to Disaster," presumably undermining the previous "monumental breakthrough" of Arab moderation toward the Jewish state, and presumably through the irresponsibility of the General Assembly.[8] But *The Times* did not see that, as the *fedayeen* triumph had Arab support, this "moderation" was very questionable. When *The Times* had occasion to deplore utterly immoderate behavior by Syria and Algeria, which were said to have been brought around to moderation by Kissinger, it made no reference to him or his policy whatever.[9]

But it was Kissinger himself who suddenly sounded the alarm that matters in the Arab world were heading in a catastrophic direction. Unless the price of oil came down drastically and fast, the world would face disaster. "Exorbitant prices can only distort the world economy, run the risk of worldwide depression and threaten the breakdown of world order and safety," warned his principal, Ford. "It is difficult to discuss the energy problem without lapsing into doomsday language."[10] A string of apparent successes of grandiose dimensions had led right up to the edge of abyss.

From October on the people were entertained by incessant celebration of miraculous advance on the entire Oriental front. True, the Israelis were troubled, but that was the price of abandoning their myths. "Elsewhere," concluded a typical assessment in the following spring, "the Middle East picture seemed to be growing brighter. Israeli and Egyptian forces along the Suez Canal front completed their disengagement ahead of schedule and without a single significant clash. Plans for the Israeli-Syrian disengagement negotiations—to be conducted in Washington through the good offices of Secretary of State Henry Kissinger—were still on track, and American officials indicated the talks might begin next week, after Kissinger returns from his tentative trip to Moscow. What's more, the U.S. could take some satisfaction in watching the Soviets scramble to regain some of the influence in the Arab world that Kissinger had stolen with his virtuoso diplomacy. And finally, the Arab oil embargo against the U.S. was expected to be lifted early this week—removing one more obstacle to what appears to be a remarkable rapprochement between the U.S. and the Arabs."[11]

Then Kissinger made the oil flow once more and his continuing efforts for peace in the Middle East and special relationship with Arab leaders would assure abundant and uninterrupted streams of oil to us and our Western allies. He had indicated in private conversations that the Arab-Israeli settlement he sought, mainly on Arab terms, "not only would bring peace to the Mideast but would end the worldwide oil crisis. For Saudi Arabia has offered to boost its oil production to 20 million barrels a day once the United States can guarantee an Israeli pullback behind the 1967 boundaries. This would be twice the eight million barrels that came out of Saudi oil fields daily before the Yom Kippur war."[12] *That*, all of a sudden, turned out to be precisely the disaster: the enormously overpriced glut of oil was fast draining the industrial world of its lifeblood.

American foreign policy under Kissingerian tutorship had somehow managed to mistake the real nature of the "energy crisis" from the first. The problem had never been scarcity and access, but collusion among producers: create artificial shortages and enormously high prices. Far from being a secret, this was publicly argued and documented as soon as the matter became a popular issue, by Professor M. A. Adelman of M.I.T., challenging the Akins version, named after the leading State Department oil expert, which our foreign policy adopted.[13] As monopoly, the oil producers were in effect engaged in economic warfare against the oil importers, chiefly the West, but were in that capacity also greatly vulnerable. But the State Department, Adelman indicated, had itself all along acquiesced in, and strengthened, the oil companies and producing countries' ability to maintain monopoly prices. And the press, with Akins in the lead and the oil companies in an unprecedented public relations campaign, were in fact telling a near-hysterical country that the game was up, that America and the West were already at the mercy of Saudi Arabia and other Arab states, that there was nothing one could do but appease them, by throwing Israel into their "peace." The State Department was apologizing for the Arabs and their agents in our oil companies, indeed enjoying their self-fulfilled prophecy.[14] For had State not all along warned that failure to cheer the Arabs went counter to vital American interests?

Kissinger's actions in the October War and after were clearly consistent with this policy of humoring the nemesis of one's own making. The conceptualizer was in this respect as conformist to State Department dogma as in other aspects of Middle Eastern affairs. Unlike other aspects, there was here a public consensus of the elite of American economists against the policy, the unusual intervention by four Nobel laureates and other leading specialists on November 20, 1973, going unheeded by the former Harvard professor. But if overrated as conceptualizer, he surely surprised in apparently failing as one who understands politics and power. If anyone did not grasp that this was "war," the chief spokesman for the oil producing countries, Sheikh Ahmed Zaki al-Yamani of Saudi Arabia, himself made this unmistakable, publicly saying so for all to know.[15] Certainly Henry Kissinger could not possibly fail to understand that; hence his actions under the circumstances must reveal much about his mettle in a struggle and would seem to confirm the impression of Ronald Steel, Arthur Schlesinger and many others, that he shrinks from confrontation with America's enemies and antagonizes her friends. His performance in the Middle East thus raises grave doubts as to whether his more grandiose policies on the global scale represented imaginative thinking. The disturbing observations on Henry Kissinger's personality by those who know him intimately, cited in an earlier chapter, thus assume added significance.

While the Arabs' war on the West gathered momentum, Kissinger moved to confront Israel, not merely throwing away an ace, but giving the Arabs the added momentum of military exultation and success and assuring their exploiting the United States with impunity. The fate of the West was to hinge on the Arabs' goodwill and reasonableness. Expressed to many, his rationale of policy was well summarized soon after the October War by Jack Anderson: "He is convinced that Egypt's President Anwar Sadat and Saudi Arabia's King Faisal are sincere in their offer to accept the pre-1967 Israel. As Kissinger sees it, Sadat and Faisal are moderates who want nothing more than to stop the rise of radicals and the spread of Soviet influence in the Arab world. Already Sadat, with the support of Faisal's oil billions, has thrown out Soviet military advisers. But the two leaders know they can never sell their brand of moderation to the Arab world unless they lead the crusade to recover the lost Arab lands. The Yom Kippur attack and the subsequent diplomatic offensive have won them widespread Arab support. They want to use this, Kissinger believes, to rally the Arab nations around a reasonable and responsible Mideast settlement. By using the oil valves as a political weapon, King Faisal has made the world dance to the Arab tune. But he is aware, in Kissinger's view, that the Western world will unite against him if he tightens the oil vise too tight. Therefore, he is willing to listen to reason."[16]

The Saudi Arabian response gave every indication of vindicating the faith. Sheikh al-Yamani repeatedly impressed American audiences with his moderation; Saudi delegates to O.P.E.C.

meetings were invariably said to favor lower pricing of oil. Secretary Simon's confident predictions that oil prices would soon come down became something of a ritual in news reporting. But prices did not come down, and it took almost a year for Kissinger and his principal to discern the pattern. Even after the alarm and doomsday language before the United Nations and elsewhere, presumably in the realization that the campaign to bring the cost of oil down had failed conspicuously, the Secretary went to Saudi Arabia to elicit yet another expression of intent to work for a lower world oil price, the King encouraging him to publicize these intentions, which he did. Newsmen traveling with the Secretary were advised not to expect that the Saudis would act unilaterally. Rather, they were told, the King would try to persuade other members of the Organization of Petroleum Exporting Countries, such as Iran, to make joint price reductions. "Thus," wrote one observer, "it is a familiar scenario that is unrolling—with the King cast as Good Guy and the Shah of Iran as Bad Guy—and it remains to be seen whether this particular drama will be any more productive than the last."[17] At the next O.P.E.C. meeting, the price was increased still more. Kissinger's immediate response to the realization of failure in the oil cost campaign was both panicky and counterproductive. The vehemence and desperation with which he and Ford sounded the alarm frightened Arab oil producers, but they quickly realized that there was no bite in the bark. There was merely to be an appeal to their charity and an attempt at rallying the Western nations to some mild reduction of oil imports and equalization of financial burdens, none of which apparently caused them to lose much sleep. The hard new line Washington took in public in September of 1974 thus indicated frustration and a sense of impotence, as did the subsequent reference to the use of "force" in Kissinger's *Business Week* (January 13, 1975) interview. Yet despite failure, the reliance on Arab moderation persisted.

The trouble with this policy was that it excluded all but catastrophic alternatives to failure. Means short of military intervention had to be either ignored or used with insufficient credibility for as long as one courted the Arabs, leaving only terrifying measures in the end. "Congressmen grumble," Evans and Novak reported, "that Kissinger has engaged in sabre-rattling against oil-producing states while flinching at the use of economic countermeasures."[18] A grim mood had indeed been spreading in Washington for some time. "One important policymaker," reported Jack Anderson, "in confidential talks with us, compared the oil gouge to Pearl Harbor. In fact, he assessed the economic damage as far greater than what resulted from the bombing of Pearl Harbour. The Arab oil rulers, he insisted, are engaged in overt economic warfare. They have used oil as a weapon to demand political concessions. They have even imposed wartime secrecy upon their oil strategy meetings he said. In the backrooms, Secretary of State Kissinger has opposed even hinting at military action against the Arabs. He has confidence that the Arab moderates, particularly Egypt's President Sadat and Saudi Arabia's King Faisal, can restore oil prices to a let-live level. U.S. military intervention, he has warned, could set the entire Middle East on fire."[19] The tragic irony is that he might well have insured that this would indeed happen.

Given the extraordinary relationship of the press to Kissinger, there was hardly much public realization of his role. Indeed, the more likely impression for the public was that he had discovered a critical situation and was working assiduously to rally our allies to meet it. Only a rare dissenter would want to know where Kissinger had been all these many years in which the crisis was abuilding. "One reason that there has been inadequate attention to [the deeper issues of our time] is that they have not happened to interest the man who alone makes American foreign policy," answered Anthony Lewis. "After a year of selling arms to the Persian Gulf states and parading Richard Nixon through the streets of Cairo, Mr. Kissinger has suddenly discovered that the price of Arab oil is too high. We should not have had to wait for him."[20] But there was still no public debate, even then. And should the Arab moderates continue to disappoint, and Kissinger still be around for the perhaps inevitable explosion, chances were that he would probably argue that his promising policy had been sabotaged by reactionary and militaristic circles. (The Rabat setback has been blamed by Kissinger on—Israel.)[21]

The fiasco on petroleum highlights the nature of the vaunted breakthrough to the Arab world, the achievement of American influence at Soviet expense. Within a year of the celebrated feat, the influence seemed rather to be Arab influence over the United States, the Russians were back stirring Arab affairs and Brezhnev was expected to tour Egypt, Syria and other Arab states sometime in 1975. The Kissinger breakthrough was eroding so fast for the simple reason that, though there was an illusion of it, it was never achieved in the first place. In the last resort, there was triumph because Kissinger himself said so, and as usual the press conveyed this to the people as fact, incessantly and with adulation. "Mr. Kissinger has won the confidence of President Sadat and King Faisal," announced James Reston. "The domination of Arab policy by the Soviet Union has been broken. . . ."[22] The Russians were scrambling, *Newsweek* said, "to regain some of the influence in the Arab world that Kissinger had stolen with his virtuoso diplomacy."[23] As late as June of 1974, *The Times* man in the Kissinger entourage celebrated the "Arab Turn to the West" on its front page, revealing some of the thinking in that circle, or the "optimistic reasoning," as he terms it.

"American officials," wrote Bernard Gwertzman, "have refrained from talking about it publicly, but many of them say privately that Secretary of State Kissinger's persistence in bringing about the Syrian-Israeli disengagement agreement will open the way for the United States to displace the Soviet Union as the major foreign influence in the Arab world. . . . As part of this optimistic reasoning, improved Arab-American relations would inevitably be translated into increased prestige for the moderate leaders in the Arab world and a drop in the power of the radicals who for so many years have dominated the Arab political scene. Hopefully, the Americans believe that this would increase the chances for a peaceful resolution of the Arab-Israeli conflict. The prospects of this development, which would end America's near isolation for two decades in the Arab world, have fascinated Mr. Kissinger and his top aides, though they have been hesitant to draw attention to them for fear of causing increased and unwanted friction with the Soviet Union. But it has been impossible to travel with Mr. Kissinger through his five Middle East trips since November—including the 33-day journey which ended early this morning—without noting the increased warmth for the United States, expressed not only by such moderates as President Anwar el-Sadat of Egypt but also by so-called 'radicals' such as President Hafez al-Assad of Syria. . . . One of the things that intrigued Mr. Kissinger and his aides through the long days and nights of negotiating with the Syrians was the strong sign received that Damascus, unhappy being known as Moscow's main client in the area, strongly desired to follow Mr. Sadat's example and move toward a more balanced policy between East and West.

"Washington officials believe that if the Arab countries follow this moderate trend the United States will become the prime foreign influence in the area because only America has the vast markets, capital and technology sought by virtually every Arab nation. Until recently, Americans have been so linked with Israel in the eyes of the Arab world that any initiatives by Washington were suspect. But the dramatic shifts in attitude, precipitated by Mr. Kissinger's shuttle diplomacy, have won for the United States such a reputation for fairness, goodwill and—in Mr. Kissinger's case—success that Mr. Nixon will be traveling to the Middle East at a time of unparalleled opportunity."[24]

It is a measure of the intellectual climate in the Kissingerian period that such self-indulgence can be mistaken for realpolitik. Note the minuteness of the factual basis from which the wishful thinking takes off in flights of fancy. At any rate, the test of "influence" is the capacity to make others meet United States' needs without force, not merely America's ministering to theirs. Kissinger's achievement consists in the latter, not the former. The United States was rebuffed, even when it termed its needs vital, but was expected to supply the Arabs' without letup. The Arabs did not yield to the United States on oil, the Palestinians and virtually all other important issues. But in turn they were quite willing to let America give them Israeli retreats, financial aid, food, nuclear technology, naval assistance in clearing the Suez Canal and more. They offer "warmth" to visiting American diplomats for so long as the gifts are forthcoming. There was a notable drop in their "warmth" on the occasion of Kissinger's tour of the Arab world late in 1974, which Arabs explained by asking, what he had done for them lately: there were no new Israeli retreats, and the promised financial gifts were slow in coming.[25] When one realizes that this "warmth" is in effect quite spontaneously available even to enemies visiting Arabs, since hospitality is a supreme value among them and they are known to bestow "friendship" upon virtual strangers, the irony of the United States diplomatic achievement is even more obvious. When the previous Secretary of State Rogers visited Sadat for the first and only time during a low point in American-Arab relations, he was immediately greeted as "Dear Bill" for exchanges that were as affectionate as they were fruitless. And the impressive sounding claim, to have won the "confidence" of Arab leaders, was equally meaningless as influence for the same reason. It evoked visions of the Pied Piper of Hamlin; whereas Arab leaders explained that they trusted him to satisfy *their* needs.

The lack of sensitivity to American desiderata was demonstrated long before Rabat and even earlier disappointments, indeed in the heady period immediately following Syrian disengagement, in the affair of the Khartoum murderers of our diplomats. In one of their familiar actions, eight Palestinian gunmen on March 1, 1973, entered the Saudi Arabian embassy in the capital of the Sudan and seized several diplomats attending a farewell party for American Ambassador George Moore. After releasing their Arab hostages, they savagely beat and abused

Moore, his successor Cleo Noel Jr., and the Belgian charge d'affaires Guy Eid, finally murdering them in the basement of the embassy. The gunmen claimed to represent a dissident *fedayeen* group, the Black September, but the Sudanese quickly traced them to the official P.L.O. offices in Khartoum. Arafat himself had supervised the staging of this assassination.

If the outrage had taken place in the bad old days, before relations between Khartoum and Washington were re-established, the perpetrators would have been released to the custody of the P.L.O. and flown to another Arab country, probably Egypt, to be sheltered free. But now things were supposed to be different. Formal relations had been set anew in 1972. President Gaafar al-Numeiri was supposedly a moderate who sought to steer a Sudanese course untrammeled by the incendiary lures of Arabism. America quickly rewarded him with aid, an $11 million loan for agricultural development, a $2.2 million grant for refugee assistance, and a $2.1 million long term, low interest loan for the purchase of 20,000 tons of wheat.

The first Sudanese response to the Palestinian outrage seemed to confirm America's hopeful evaluations. President al-Numeiri condemned the perpetrators as cowardly murderers, promising stern justice. The P.L.O. office in Khartoum was closed by the Sudanese authorities and *fedayeen* broadcasts from Radio Omdurman were halted. The Palestinians were held for trial. Meanwhile, the improvement in relations with the Arab world spurted to new heights, with the descent of Kissinger on the Middle East in the wake of the October War, the triumphal tour of Nixon in the area and a veritable avalanche of new aid offers and political commitments to cement the new friendship.

A test of the new Arab attitude followed on the heels of Nixon's consummation of the historic shift, on June 25, 1974. Exactly as in the old days—the sameness was almost incredible —all the eight Palestinian murderers of the American diplomats were set free and flown to Egypt. The State Department was stunned, as if struck by lightning, officially "dismayed," in utter disbelief of this sample of the "new" relationship with the Arabs.[26]

The immediate reaction was one of anger: anger at having been duped by the Sudanese, who had promised repeatedly to punish the murderers severely (their President personally pledged it); anger at having played down the affair for so long in order to accommodate the Sudan's political expediency, and for nothing (earlier in the year the Sudan allowed the P.L.O. to reopen offices in Khartoum and resume broadcasting over the state radio); anger at the insensitivity to American feelings—even in Sadat's Egypt—for here, after all, the matter touched not just some children in a Jewish settlement, but their very own, foreign service officers and Arabists, to boot; anger at the revelation of their powerlessness vis-à-vis "their" Arabs, who did not bother to consult or even advise them. ("American officials," said one press report, "were indignant today at the apparent failure of the Saudi Government to put pressure on the Sudanese to punish the men," who are on the Saudi payroll, after all.)

But rather than draw the implications for the worth of the new-won influence among Arabs, the United States diplomats scrambled to apologize for the outrage in order to secure it. The Khartoum action, "informed officials" explained, "indicated the pressures to which leaders of Middle East nations are subjected by the radical Palestinian organization."[27] But the apology itself was troubling, for did it not mean that extremists have the power to commit moderates in the Arab world against their will (assuming the questionable proposition that the latter do not share the emotional compulsions of the former)?

United States diplomacy went into high gear, and at week's end, June 29, 1974, *The New York Times* front page announced that Egypt had actually jailed the murderers freed by Khartoum. Had we been falsely alarmed? Not really, according to the fine print below the headline. It seems that our ambassador in Cairo had raised the matter with the Egyptian Foreign Minister, not to confront him with grave doubts, but rather with solicitude, "for fear of upsetting Egypt." What the

United States wanted was a gesture, to protect aid to Egypt from the wrath of Congress and the Foreign Minister gave as much, so that the State Department could aver that *according to him* the Palestinians were in jail. The nature of this "jailing" was immediately clarified, since Egypt would absolutely not bring the murderers to trial, but rather ship them to yet another Arab country for safe haven. And five months later the man accused by Gaafar al-Numeiri as chief planner of the assassination reportedly came to New York in the party of Arafat for the United Nations General Assembly session. The presence of Fawaz Yassin Abd al-Rahman, who had been head of the P.L.O. offices in Khartoum and flew to Lybia just hours before the attack, was announced by both British and American sources.[28] The State Department could not deny it, but showed little interest in the matter beyond stating that his name was not on the P.L.O. delegation list, presumably to protect its "influence" in the Arab world.

At year's end on December 13, 1974 came yet another toughening of the Arab posture that stunned Washington. Egypt had been thought to offer a peaceful agreement in return for total Israeli withdrawal and the establishment of a P.L.O. regime in Palestine. Suddenly, Foreign Minister Fahmi added further staggering conditions: Israel would have to suspend immigration for the next fifty years and withdraw still further, to the partition lines envisaged in 1947. Since this spelled national suicide no less clearly than the P.L.O. program, officials in Jersusalem at first refused to comment, believing that Fahmi must have been misquoted. Several days after the text was confirmed, Jerusalem learned that Washington was determined to deliver the nuclear reactor that Egypt had been promised earlier.

14. The Fate of the West

An interesting aspect of Henry Kissinger's Middle East policy was that it was not particularly Kissingerian. Seeking American hegemony and peace in the area by wooing the Arabs with Israeli-held territory was an ancient State Department approach, indeed the only one it ever really knew and approved. Lest one mistake the pressure for Israeli withdrawal as occasioned by the unprecedented circumstance of the Jewish state's holding large occupied areas since 1967, it must be recalled that the same approach was pressed by the State Department before. The several American proposals for peace since 1948 invariably envisaged some cession of land from Israel proper in return for Arab acceptance (and amity for America).

Under the leadership of John Foster Dulles, who nearly matched Henry Kissinger in his autonomy in foreign policy and also concentrated heavily on Middle Eastern affairs, the State Department pressed with particular vigor a campaign to capture Nasser for an anti-Soviet alliance in conjunction with a settlement with Israel, the plan featuring amputation of large areas in the south of that country. Like Kissinger, Dulles had started his campaign for Arab good will with a grand tour of the Arab world, stressing his readiness to satisfy the Arabs in defiance of the Zionist lobby at home. The campaign abutted in the entrenchment of the Soviet Union in Egypt and the subsequent preemptive strike by Israel in the fall of 1956 into the Sinai. Washington's reaction to that was once again, pressure for Israeli withdrawal (for which soon enough the Arabs credited the Soviet Union) and some Arab promises and American guarantees that proved worthless, preparing the way for yet another war.

The rigid adherence to bankrupt policy in the Middle East derives in essence from an ideological outlook in the State Department that has more to do with the Protestant missionary experience than the reality of that part of the world. American Protestant missionaries went to the Middle East over one hundred and fifty years ago, establishing the main American "interest" there for nearly a century. Having failed to convert virtually anyone to Christianity, they stayed to minister to Arab nationalism, forever apologizing for it and "explaining" it at home with what Elie Kedourie termed the "Missionary Version" of Islam and the Arab world, a patronizing interpretation that distorts their essence.[1] It regards as some brand of liberal Protestantism one of the most politically aggressive civilizations in history, sharing neither the code of personal conduct and social morality of the West nor its concepts of international order.

The missionaries colonized the Middle Eastern departments of the United States foreign office and academies and even now men with missionary (or other ecclesiastic) and diplomatic affiliations control virtually all the institutions identified with expertise in Middle Eastern affairs (such as the Middle East Institute, Friends of the Middle East, Holy Land Center, etc.). While their influence on the State Department is said to be weaker, their role as its ideologists persists.[2] The irony has been that the persisting dominance by men with but superficial linguistic and other knowledge of the Arab world and Islam has been justified by their "expertise," since they are the "Arabists." And because of their other institutional domination, they are accepted as such by the larger grouping of political scientists and foreign policy analysts who lack adequate training in Oriental affairs. Since they misunderstand their subject at the core, their dismal record was all but inevitable, but they have a standard excuse in an unsufficiently supportive public opinion at home. They are always right; what is wrong is domestic politics responding to popular desiderata. Even if their understanding of the Arabs and Islam were adequate, any definition of national interest at odds with the political system itself could hardly make for good policy abroad.

Lacking an independent, thorough knowledge of the Middle East, Henry Kissinger was not likely to reject the State Department thinking, even if his psychological need, the consuming desire for 100 per cent Americanism, had not inclined him to identify with it in any case. For despite its narrowly sectarian origin, that line is presented as the non-hyphenated, true American posture, a perhaps irresistible appeal to anyone with such painful identity problems. His firm anti-Zionism goes back at least to his Harvard student days. In fact, few bureaus in the State Department have enjoyed such close and warm working relations with Secretary Kissinger as that which houses the "Arabists," whose elitist disdain for domestic politics he shares and with whom he has had close contacts throughout his earlier career. Yet these Bureau of Near Eastern Affairs officials, with their similar pro-Arab anti-Zionist sentiments, are more likely to encourage his idiosyncracies than to check them.

A man already exuding competitiveness with the Soviet Union finds in the Near East Bureau conviction that the Arab world is a particularly suitable and vital area for such struggle. The Bureau is traditionally concerned with Soviet advances in that part of the world to the point of obsession and full of such dicta as, "A vibrant Arab nationalism is the best shield against Soviet penetration," and similar clichés. A man who lacks anything but confidence in his diplomatic skills finds in the Bureau the conviction at all times that the time for the elusive Arab-Israeli settlement is at hand, if only a gifted statesman could master refractory domestic interference long enough to pull it off. For despite their meaningless public noises, the Arabs out there are really moderate and ready for a final solution, except that one must allow for their domestic political needs when they appear to stray from the commitments given in private. The "Arabist" translation of Arab words and intent is invariably optimistic, finding hope even in unambiguous negativism.

One can gather from their known record what sort of interpretation State Department advisers are likely to give to their Secretary in his tours of the Arab world. Nearly thirty years ago they coached private Americans on a diplomatic mission in the Middle East to discount the bristling hostility and threats to Zionism expressed to them by King Saud, since the King spoke merely for the record and actually opposed violent resistance to the Jews' enterprise in Palestine.[3] A quarter of a century of almost unceasing violence later Secretary Rogers was told in similar terms by another Saudi monarch that Israel is an abomination and his advisers afterward explained that the King is actually reconciled to Israel already.[4] When Nasser came to power, the "Arabists" checked him out and declared him relatively unhostile to Israel; when Sadat succeeded Nasser, two wars with Israel later, they cleared him, too. They are consistent and predictable.

A vital corrective to Kissinger's characteristic rational gamesmanship in international politics is not to be forthcoming from the Bureau. Like all games, this presupposes a sharing of concepts of conduct, which simply does not obtain in Western-Muslim interaction. Few cross-cultural dealings are indeed so difficult and perilous. "Rationality" in the Arab context is very different from that of the United States, as are other pivotal conceptions lacking precise or even proximate equivalence. This is understood by the rare genuine Orientalist in the service of the State Department, but the typical "Arabist" is an amateur whose notion of empathy for Arabs is support rather than imaginative projection of one's consciousness into others.

When such a man, Harold Glidden, spoke not long ago on the Arab-Israeli conflict, as cited in an earlier chapter, his observations challenged the State Department posture at its very base. He made especially clear the fact that the conflict was above all else an extraordinary one. What is ironic is that Henry Kissinger had as a private writer taken great care to warn his readers against mistaking just such a conflict for an

ordinary one. He did not discover the distinction, for it is known at least since Edmund Burke; and his teacher, Hans Morgenthau, has stressed it in his writing. He termed "imperialistic" those conflicts involving the overthrow of the status quo, rather than adjustments within the existing order. Kissinger's critique of "non-revolutionary" states in dealing with a "revolutionary" power could hardly apply more to his own State Department's (and his own) approach to the Arab-Israeli conflict. "They would not accept the impasse for what it was; they wanted to believe that the "revolutionary' state was simply exaggerating its position so that it might achieve certain tactical gains. Confident that limited concessions would in time produce a 'thaw,' which would contribute to a willingness to discuss fundamental issues, they insisted that the end result would be agreement. Non-revolutionary states, Kissinger wrote, found it hard to accept the proposition that other states could have 'unlimited objectives,' and that these objectives were non-negotiable. The idea that 'revolutionary' states had no interest in adjudicating differences—that their principal purpose was to subvert loyalties—was difficult for a non-revolutionary state to accept. When an international system included a 'revolutionary' state, and when that state was powerful, Kissinger explained, an arms race or war was the general result."[5] Clearly, Secretary Kissinger refused to take the advice Professor Kissinger offered: "History demonstrates that revolutionary powers have never been brought to a halt until their opponents stopped pretending that the revolutionaries were really misunderstood legitimists."

Neither is the step-by-step approach to an Arab-Israeli settlement particularly Kissingerian. His predecessor, Secretary Rogers, had already shifted to this approach before the last war, seeking a disengagement of forces along the Suez Canal. The shift was tactical, the goal was the same: having failed to move the Israelis back to the lines held before the June War of 1967 in one fell swoop, the notion took hold quite spontaneously in many quarters that it might be possible to do it piecemeal. A Harvard law professor, Roger Fisher, who had acquired a reputation for promoting Egyptian and other Arab policy aims in this country, published an elaborate blueprint for just such a step-by-step approach in 1972 (*Dear Israelis, Dear Arabs: A Working Approach to Peace*), while others promoted it in various journals simultaneously.

The rationale for the step-by-step approach is obvious. Presenting the Israelis with the final map, as in the Rogers Plan of 1969, only frightens and antagonizes them into rigid resistance. If the pill is too large to swallow, lots of little pills will go down well. First induce the Israelis to make just one withdrawal and, having realized that the sky did not cave in afterward, they might summon courage to try yet another, and with practice the previously terrifying thought would become routine. Underlying the approach is the premise that Arabs and Israelis are separated not by incompatible aspirations but rather by misunderstanding and distrust. As they implement the various arrangements reached at each step, they would learn to trust one another and, with the process of withdrawal completed, the conflict will have melted to insubstantial size, or peace. These are the "blocks" of peace that Henry Kissinger claimed to be assembling in the Middle East.

To keep the ball rolling, Kissinger would have to persuade the Israelis that he did not indeed have a final map, that the game was open-ended and genuinely experimental. The American public would see him striving for peace without pressuring Israel to grant suicidal concessions. The Arabs understood him to share their objective of total (or virtually total) Israeli withdrawal, both Sadat and Assad publicly saying so repeatedly. His own public hints and private explanations left little doubt that his idea of a map pretty much matched the pre-June War map. If the peacemaking process proved successful, he said often, Israel would be left so weak as to require a firm American alliance for survival.

While the step-by-step approach suited an Israeli disposition to "buy" time with pieces of land, it hardly suited Jerusalem's objective in peacemaking. For its posture had been and remained readiness to exchange occupied territory for substantive concessions from the other side, meaning agreement to defensible borders and formal legitimacy to Jewish statehood. The step-by-step approach wasted the Israelis' sole bargaining chip for mere technical arrangements for implementing withdrawal and insubstantial concessions, such as demilitarization or passage of Israeli cargo through the Suez Canal, which could be (and have in the past been) nullified in an instant. On the other hand, it implemented the standing Egyptian (and other Arab) conception of "negotiation" as arranging for withdrawal according to a time table without substantive talks. By focusing only on the immediate and proximate at every step, the approach tended to circumvent Israel's crucial concerns. Pragmatism thus appeared to conceal yet another move in which Israel was cheated out of the conquests of the June War.

While acknowledging the possibility that attitudes may change in the process of diplomatic movement, Bernard Lewis warned that avoidance of purpose and ultimate concerns led to danger. "I would suggest," he told a Senate subcommittee, "that the best safeguard, as between Arab States and Israel, is a signed peace and normalization of relations. It may be objected that such a program is unrealistic and Utopian. It would be equally unrealistic and Utopian to expect the Israelis to withdraw to less defensible borders without at least some assurance that they will not have to defend them against annihilation. This, after all, is what the conflict has been about for a quarter of a century. If the threat of annihilation is real, it must be countered; if false, it must be exorcised. . . . The Arabs are often blamed for loose, wild utterances. We should, however, note the accuracy, consistency and indeed integrity of their refusal to make a real peace. In one sense this is discouraging, but it also gives some grounds for hope that once this point is  overcome, the way will really be open and not subject to sudden changes and reversals. One should not overstate the significance of diplomatic peace-making, but it seems to me that formal peace negotiations between the parties and a formal treaty of peace would have a two-fold importance. In the first place it would mean the crossing of a vital psychological barrier in the Arab world—and such crossings are not easily reversed. In the second place is would set up what the record of events in the world since 1945 has shown to be a real obstacle to armed conflict—namely, a normal, demarcated, recognized, functioning, international frontier defended by passport and customs men and traversed by regular communications. . . ."[6]

The step-by-step approach seemed almost certain of failure sooner or later since the Israelis were as unlikely to throw away their vital asset piecemeal as they were all at once previously. They might go another step or two before insisting on substantive talks that the Arabs clearly were not prepared to enter. And they could not be made to do what they did not wish to do, because of the essential contradiction in any policy reliant on extreme pressure on Israel. To break Israel's will meant weakening it to the point where the whole game was not worth the candle. If the Arabs and Russians could take from Israel what they wanted, they would no longer need the United States; indeed, a weakened Israel invited their attack and, if greatly weakened, might perhaps involve the superpowers in ominous confrontation. It was, in fact, dubious that the Congress and the people would even allow pressure to mount to such levels.

What if the Israelis were to be taken step-by-step back to the borders of 1967? Unless a radical change in Arab attitudes toward Jewish statehood also happened, the result would be just a strategically much weakened Israel. Yet such change is very unlikely to occur in such a short time. For decades of conflict have so far produced among some Arabs only a reluctant "acceptance" of the fact that an Israel is here to stay, if only for a certain period. As for guarantees and arrangements Israel might obtain, they never worked in the past and are not likely to work in future, since they are only as good as the intentions of those who implement them. In the past, arrangements for enhanced security in theory invariably became sources of insecurity when put into effect. Foreign guarantees always turned useless when really needed, because no foreign power was prepared to act decisively against the Arab world for the sake of Israel. Is this more likely to happen in future, with the Arab economic and diplomatic clout even greater than before?

Another contradiction was built right into the United States competition for Arab favor with the Russians. For vying with them for that prize was like playing with loaded dice against a United States certain to lose, no matter how hard it tried. The reason was quite simple: whatever we, the United States, might offer the Arabs at Israel's expense, the Russians could always go us one better. They could invariably outbid the United States because they have neither the domestic political nor the moral constraints that America has. They can act without regard for their Jews; public opinion and legislators and human considerations restraining even America's own pro-Arab officials. Hence while the United States strains the political system and its conscience with even initial bids for Arab favor, the Russians easily ante up without repercussions or much cost to them.

This is the simple reason why the United States policy has failed in the past and why it is bound to fail again. While Kissinger held out to Arabs the promise of regaining land lost in 1967, the Russians were already busy signalling their readiness to challenge Israel's hold on land gained before. Their propaganda in 1974 in the Arab world repeatedly insisted that much territory beyond the armistice lines of 1949 was also unlawfully held; their broadcasts in Arabic frequently reminded listeners that Soviet maps had always shown only the narrow partition lines recommended by the United Nations in 1947. They thus claimed higher ground even before Kissinger showed himself able to reach the lower. Can one imagine the United States supporting further dismemberment of Israel? The relative ease with which the Russians assumed forward positions in the competition for Arab favor was equally demonstrated in relation to the P.L.O. While the United States could not abandon Israel completely and immediately in opposition to the role accorded to the *fedayeen* both at the United Nations and at Rabat, the Russians were free to support them fully, indeed assumed a stance of sponsorship and protection toward them.

Yet another example was the American offer of a nuclear reactor to Egypt, which stirred much discontent and seemed bogged down only several months later in difficult talks concerning assurances that the device would not be used to produce atomic weapons. The Russians had no such problems or qualms, for as soon as the stalemate developed over the American offer, they announced their readiness to supply Egypt with a reactor, following this immediately with the announced readiness to supply nuclear arms to the Arabs in case Israel would be known to have any.[7]

This inherent advantage yielded the additional benefit of gaining Arab credit even for pro-Arab acts by the American competitor. The striking example is the stern posture of Eisenhower and Dulles toward Israel's conquest of the Sinai and the Gaza Strip in the 1956 war. Having first humbled the British and French for their attack on Egypt, they proceeded to force a full Israeli retreat from occupied territory. Yet within a few months, Arab gratitude was offered almost exclusively to the Russians, who had assumed during the crisis a more shrill rhetorical stance (though without American pressure the Israelis clearly would not have budged) and afterward as always quickly outbid the United States in posturing around new, evolving issues.

This explains why the Russians were not able to resist the temptation to meddle in the Middle East, the lures of détente and costly setbacks and even risk of nuclear holocaust notwithstanding. For even when they required accommodation with the United States, there remained a compulsive need to compete with America, and the Middle East offered ideal conditions for that purpose. It is instructive that their meddling in that area since détente was no less incendiary, and perhaps more, than before.

The American people were told without letup after the fall of 1973 that Egypt had broken with the Soviet Union, turning to the United States both for immediate diplomatic purposes and the shaping of the country's future. Yet there were no less than three such breaks (1959, 1961, 1972) in the last fifteen years alone, described as "irreparable," between Cairo and Moscow. Indeed, only a few months after the last of these, Sadat's "expulsion" of Soviet military personnel, the Soviet Union initiated the massive military buildup of Egypt that culminated in the October 6, 1974, attack on Israel. What explains this resilience?

The Arabs had needs that only the Soviet Union could fill, quite apart from the windfalls reaped from superpower competition for their favor. The Russians are after all the chief antagonists of the "West," that inchoate entity which in Arab consciousness epitomizes all the evil and humiliation tormenting Islam in history, particularly modern history. The depth of the animus, the intensity of which sometimes startled even Orientalists, was disguised for laymen by the almost equally avid craving among Arabs for artifacts of Western civilization and the prestige of Western-type education. The *personal* preference for Westerners thus comes as naturally as the spontaneous anti-Western posture in politics, but our policy makers have steadfastly confused the two. (The latest Arab "turn" to the West was thus explained by the observation that Egyptians did not much like Russians.)

"The simple fact of the matter," states a report of a Washington symposium on October 21–22, 1974, co-authored by this writer, exposing the other side of Moscow's independent hold on the Arabs, "is that the Egyptian régime rests essentially upon the support of its armed forces, both domestically and in terms of Egypt's hegemonial aspirations over the Middle East as a whole. These Egyptian forces have been habituated by Moscow to a standard of military consumption, both qualitatively and quantitatively, that the U.S. could not support if it would. The statistics speak for themselves: within a few years, the U.S.S.R. supplied Egypt, Syria, Iraq, and Algeria with armor equal to almost 10 times the current U.S. annual tank production. Moreover, there are whole Soviet weapons systems in which the U.S., for perfectly valid reasons has not specialized, such as the S.A.M. 2, 3, 6, 7 series. Consequently, the U.S. could not replace the U.S.S.R. as Egypt's main arms supplier, even if, for the sake of argument, such a policy were to be considered rational. In any case, even if America were physically capable of adopting this role of Cairo's primary weapons suppliers, such a change-over could not prove acceptable to the Egyptian forces: weapons systems are produced to serve specific military doctrines and it would be militarily absurd to change weapons systems without a corresponding alteration in strategic doctrine. However, while a MIG pilot might be retrained to fly a Phantom in a matter of months, members of the Egyptian military staff would require a much longer period to relearn their Frunze Academy indoctrination and to be taught anew at Fort Leavenworth. In the intervening period of such a hypothetical change-over, 18 months or more, the Egyptian armed forces would, to all intents and purposes, be out of action. It is simply inconceivable that these forces, and a régime intimately linked to them and needing them, both as an arm and threat symbol of Egyptian policy, would willingly allow such a situation to arise. Thus, there is no feasible alternative, from the Egyptian view, to the U.S.S.R. as a main arms supplier. Recently history shows, indeed, that after each political disagreement with Moscow, sooner or later Cairo has always come back with a plea to its Soviet weapons donor to renew arms shipments, and the U.S.S.R. has always responded, imposing terms of its own, needless to say. This is precisely what has already begun to transpire in recent weeks. . . ."

An awareness of the Middle East's appeal to Moscow has not escaped United States policy makers in all these years, but they have persisted in drawing the wrong conclusion. Since the Russians exploit, and wax on, the Arab-Israeli conflict, they argue, the United States must intensify efforts to solve it. So they have redoubled their pressure on Israel for a settlement (having little if any leverage on the other side), thus intensifying the very competition with Moscow they are seeking to end. The Kissinger Middle East offensive was just another replay of what may be termed a neurotic bid for yet more punishment. The pattern was already evident around the first anniversary of the launching of the "new" United States policy, as more and more observers were beginning to notice that, far from being out in the cold, where the offensive supposedly pushed them, the Russians were actually very much inside, indeed," in the catbird seat," as C. L. Sulzberger saw it.[8]

Like the neurotic who has learned to seek relief from depression by washing his hands, our policy makers have kept running to the faucet as soon as depression returned, inevitably. Having "evicted" the Russians from Egypt with Israeli concessions just a few months before, they were reported again pressing Israel for more, in anxious anticipation of Brezhnev's visit of Cairo. The idea was quickly to give Egypt another slice of the Sinai, to induce it not to bring the Russians in on the negotiations. One had virtually to press this gift on Egypt and United States officials were described as anxious lest publicity of the affair would embarrass Egypt into refusing to take it. The certainty of ultimate failure could be garnered from a Cairo report on the morrow,[9] indicating that the Russians and many others would eventually have to be brought in to assure Egypt's full satisfaction: "Mr. Fahmy also made it clear that the Government of President Anwar el-Sadat wanted the Ford Administration to continue its mediation attempts. 'What other country can force Israel to withdraw?' he asked." But, as the Egyptians had said all along, since domestic considerations restrained America from applying the coercion necessary to break Israel's determination to keep in the end some essential territory and not to bargain with the *fedayeen*, the Russians and the other powers in Europe and elsewhere were absolutely vital in pushing the United States over that line, both by pressure on the United States and by military aid to enable the Arabs to threaten war.

As soon as it appeared that Kissinger may be failing, the thinking in the foreign policy community switched to yet another failed nostrum. Since one could not keep the Russians out, it was reasoned, one must seek agreement with them on a common plan and impose it jointly on the Middle Eastern nations. That this was yet another chance for the Russians to compete with the United States on their terms, seemed not to have occurred to United States statesmen, who curiously ignored the fact that the ploy had been American policy several years before. After conceding virtually in all respects to the Soviet-Arab posture, the United States, having discovered that Moscow held out for still more, abandoned the policy in 1970. Agreement with the Russians could come on their terms only after which they would be free to press for additional concessions.

The irony in all this is that the United States had enormous strength in dealing in the Middle East, but its policy makers insisted on playing United States weaknesses instead. America had in that part of the world three pivotal and strong supporters in Ethiopia, Iran and Israel—all natural allies of the United States and of each other for reasons going to the very core of their consciousness and even existence, not the fickle "friends" in the Arab world who required incessant bribing by the highest bidder. The Middle East is not only not overwhelmingly Arab (contrary to the popular misconception, it is only about half Arab in population), but the substantial powers in the region are mostly non-Arab, and even anti-Arab in various degrees. Iran, with a population as large as Egypt's, the most populous Arab state, and territory nearly twice the size of Egypt, dominates the strategically important Persian Gulf, where the largest oil deposits in the world are believed to exist. Though Muslim, Iran is not Arab and has engaged in almost permanent warfare with adjacent Arab Iraq. Unlike most Arabs, the Iranians are Shiite Muslims, not Sunnite Muslims; in Iraq, the Shiite half of the population is under the heel of the Sunnite half, a condition which only aggravates the geopolitical confrontation. The Iranians feel almost as threatened by pan-Arabism as the Israelis and they invariably oppose Egypt and any other Arab state that happens to promote the movement..

Israel is situated at the crossroads of three continents in the eastern end of the Mediterranean, featuring in that equally vital strategic location overwhelming military power on a scientific and industrial base unmatched in the entire region. Feeling threatened by Soviet imperialism, like Iran, the Jewish state turns to the West, but in its case there exists also a natural affinity with the West on cultural and other grounds. Hence a tacit alliance exists between Iran and Israel, supported not by sentiment so much as by mutuality of vital interest. Iran and Israel have cooperated closely on petroleum, trade, technical assistance and military affairs. On the other hand, Israel has developed similar ties with Ethiopia, a large and populous state situated also in a vital spot, astride the Red Sea, south of the Sudan. As Iran does, Ethiopia cooperates closely also with the United States in military and other matters. The natural affinity of Ethiopia with Israel is similar to Iran's in that this Christian polity is surrounded by Muslims on virtually all sides and engages in permanent warfare with the Arab-backed Eritrean insurgents. The link to Israel is in this case supported also both by historical myth and reality, namely the traditional account that the ruling line was founded by King Solomon's son by the Queen of Sheba and the authentic thirteen hundred years of Christian survival in a hostile Muslim environment.

Far from building on this strength, the Arab orientation of the United States State Department has tended to liquidate it. Attempts by defense and intelligence officials to build on this strength were eventually frustrated by American diplomacy, which went into high gear with Kissinger after the fall of 1973. It is instructive that since that recent date, one of the pivots, Ethiopia, has plunged into chaos and what appeared to be perhaps even national disintegration, having been virtually abandoned by the United States already in 1971. Another, Israel was pushed into a critical situation. Perhaps Iran escaped this fate because of its enormous oil riches, but was pushed against Israel by Washington's own erosion of support for the Jewish state. In its exultation over Kissinger's "winning" of Egypt, the press has scarcely noted the waste of genuine American strength in that part of the world.

Equally wasted is the considerable strength America possesses also in the Arab part of the Middle East. For the "Arabists" are quite right when they cite the attraction to Arabs of United States technology, trade and educational facilities. But they are wrong in their claim that Arabs are somehow doing the United States a favor in satisfying these needs, that America must therefore reward them for doing so. Arabs have shown that they will not deprive themselves of American lures even when they count the United States to be hostile to their cherished goals. In what was probably the longest low period in American-Arab relations so far, between the wars of 1967 and 1973, the absence of even formal diplomatic relations with several Arab states did not prevent informal relations, at times more intense than under normal conditions; neither did Arab students cease coming in large numbers to United States universities in America or in their own countries; nor did trade suffer much, in fact gaining substantially in some cases, as with Algeria, over previous levels; and American technology, medicine and even fashion did not lose any standing in the Arab world either. In few other things has the still compulsive missionary approach to the Arabs betrayed itself more in State Department thinking than in its presumption that the United States must be grateful for their allowing it to give them all these goods.

What does the United States get in return for its steadfast support of several Arab regimes? The fact that it ranges from important to vital is yet another unproductive asset for critical American concerns. The United States is practically the guarantor of the Saudi monarchy, which yet wages calamitous war on the United States and the West with the "oil weapon." How could the Rabat summit strike a unanimous blow at America's anxious Middle East diplomacy with Saudi Arabia, Tunisia, Jordan, Morocco, Lebanon and other "friends" in its midst?

The Arabs of course fully realize America's pivotal position in their confrontation with the Jewish state. For if the United States fully backs it, they know their frustration is total. There is no way—economically, politically, militarily—that they can move Israel, unless America lets them. Together, the United States and Israel are virtually immune to any combination of forces in the Arabs' behalf. America is only marginally dependent on Arab oil and the political cost for full backing of

Israel is less than unbearable. It only *sounds* scary that the United States finds itself "isolated" in the United Nations at Israel's side, but there is little real bite to the rhetoric. For virtually all the states voting against the United States would not allow this to interfere in all their other relations with America. Knowing this full well, the Arabs endeavor to separate the United States from the Jewish state, using war scares, pressure on others to pressure America, various inducements and a host of other tactics. Indeed, America was never so ardently pursued by the Arabs as in the few years after the June War, when the United States found itself practically underwriting Israel's posture, however reluctantly. The real United States influence among Arabs, and its prestige vis-à-vis Moscow was probably never higher than then. For America's failure to budge, however brief, brought home to the Arabs painfully the lesson that no amount of Russian diplomatic and military support can impress the Israelis, when really backed by the United States.

Characteristically, American policy makers could not wait to waste this asset as well. With Henry Kissinger's arrival at the State Department, the silent chafing under the yoke of the status quo and the quiet craving for "movement" was given new sound and energy. As he himself told the leading Egyptian editor Haikal after the war, he was almost grateful for the Arabs' upset making it possible for him to play the role he had for so long yearned to fill. The compulsion to play games with the Russians transforms this asset into coin with which to vie for Arab favor. How much of the latter will the United States get for "delivering" Israel, now that America's unique capacity to do so has been acknowledged? (The brief interlude merely proved that American backing of Israel frustrated the Arabs, not that the United States could really "deliver" to the Arabs all they want from Israel.)

It would be irresponsible to claim that continued full backing for Israel would soon have brought peace to the Middle East, because this blessed state may not be achievable in the near future, no matter what. But the Kissingerian offensive may set back what chances there were for peace in the Middle East by perhaps as much as a generation. For unless peace comes to that region on the grave of Jewish statehood, the Arabs' genuine accommodation to it is more unlikely than before October of 1974. The Arabs exulted over their feat in pushing the clock of history back, first to 1967, then to 1947, and have once again put the question of Israel's existence formally on the agenda of the international community. How much more bloodshed and trauma will again be required to disabuse them of expectations that only so recently were beginning to appear even to Arabs as distant as messianic dreams?

Nor would it be fair to place this burden exclusively on Kissinger's shoulders. For his "successes" were not purely public relations stunts; indeed, no such phenomena can be possible without filling some genuine sentiment in the people. But Kissinger filled some bad ones exceedingly well. They are well known to students of foreign policy, who have repeatedly cited the undaunted optimism and insufficient staying power that the American people bring to foreign affairs. The Middle East is a region where the United States might have to sustain perhaps more than elsewhere an apparently hopeless and internationally unpopular posture. Yet America's impatience showed at the very top, as when President Ford gave vent to his own, warning that "it ought to be obvious to everybody that we cannot go on indefinitely with the very delicate circumstances that exist"[10] between Israel and the Arabs. To a people craving to be universally liked, the diplomatic isolation with Israel was unusually threatening and painful. To a people insistent that no problem could withstand true application and ingenuity, the Middle East problem was particularly frustrating. Kissinger reassured all these needs, as he made the Arabs love his country, while solving an elusive problem, even without sacrifice for the long haul, for the United States could go right back to burning the oil he had made to flow abundantly to America once more. But sooner or later America would have to discover again that there is no free lunch, after all.

If the cost of Kissinger's "successes" were limited to the Arab-Israeli conflict, the United States should count itself very fortunate. For the Jews have been tested in calamity before, and with even belated United States support, will surely recover. Though the cost to them, and to America, may be terrible. But for the United States there are additional costs, because Kissinger's intervention in the Arab-Israeli conflict is inseparable from the larger process threatening the future. It is manifested in potentially disastrous economic conditions in the Western countries that might easily lead to political chaos; in heightened disunity and distrust among Western countries, and certainly in a huge appropriation of Western wealth; in growing elation and solidarity among countries hostile to the West; in America's loss of superiority and perhaps even parity relative to the Soviet Union in conventional arms and nuclear capacity; in the conquest of the United Nations and other international organizations by anti-Western coalitions; in the West's impotence before ruthless warfare through rises in the price of petroleum; in the attempts at repeating this pattern in other commodities essential to the Western style of life; in the steady erosion of the Western strategic posture in the Mediterranean, the Indian Ocean and elsewhere. Together these spell historical decline of awesome dimensions. Obviously the ingredients and some trends have been there regardless of who managed United States foreign affairs. But equally obviously the immensity of America's potential in virtually all affairs can help shape events around the world, often decisively.

Notes

Note

Chapter 1   As Seen by Arabs

1. Reported in *Le Monde*, January 28, 1974.
2. *Al-Mussawar*, July 31, 1972.
3. *Al-Akhbar*, August 19, 1973.
4. D. F. Green, ed., *Arab Theologians on Jews and Israel: Extracts from the Proceedings of the Fourth Conference of the Academy of Islamic Research*, pp. 2, 3, 13.
5. *TV Guide*, April 29, 1972, p. 33.
6. *Survey* (London), Spring, 1971, p. 172.
7. *Journal of Social Psychology*, November, 1954, pp. 240–43.
8. *Commentary*, December, 1974.
9. In the September 18, 1953 issue of *Al-Mussawar*.
10. Bernard Gwertzman, in *The New York Times*, February 25, 1974, p. 8. Ralph Blumenthal et al, *Henry Kissinger: The Private and Public Story*, p. 229.
11. "Watergate and a Jewish Secretary of State tempted the Arabs to strike in October," according to Richard Cohen, an official of the American Jewish Congress, in *The National Jewish Monthly*, January, 1974, p. 21.
12. *The New York Times*, January 24, 1974, p. 16.
13. Major General D. K. Palit, *Return to Sinai: The Arab Offensive 1973*, p. 143.

Chapter 2   As Seen by Israelis

1. Ande Manners, *Poor Cousins*, p. 62.
2. Charles Ashman, *Kissinger: The Adventures of Super-Kraut*, p. 22.
3. *Time*, October 15, 1973, p. 42.
4. Jack Anderson, in *The Washington Post*, December 16, 1973, p. B7.
5. *The New York Times*, April 26, 1974, p. 3.
6. For example, in *The New York Times*, January 16, 1974, p. 8.
7. Thus Abd al-Quddous, a close Sadat confidant, in *Akhbar al-Yom*, February 9, 1974.
8. *The New York Times*, August 21, 1974, p. 12.
9. *The New York Times*, August 22, 1974, p. 3.
10. *The New York Post*, April 30, 1974, p. 39.
11. *The New York Times*, October 16, 1974, p. 4.
12. *The New Yorker*, November 11, 1974, p. 150.
13. *New York*, December 24, 1973, p. 44.
14. *The New Leader*, December 24, 1973, p. 6.

Chapter 3   The Media: Superman

1. Max Lerner, in *The New York Post*, May 17, 1974, p. 53.
2. *The New York Times*, May 11, 1974, p. 31, excerpted from his article, "Henry Kissinger and the Media: A Separate Peace," in *Columbia Journalism Review*, May/June, 1974, where further quotations are found.
3. *The New York Times*, June 21, 1974, p. 37.
4. June 11, 1974, p. 40.
5. *The New York Times*, August 11, 1974, Section 4, p. 4.
6. On "Behind the Lines," WNET Channel 13 Newark, November 29, 1974.
7. Leslie Gelb, in *The New York Times*, April 21, 1974, p. 16.
8. On "Behind the Lines," above.
9. *The New York Times*, November 18, 1974, p. 11.
10. Blumenfeld, *Henry Kissinger*, p. 15.
11. Stephen Graubard, *Kissinger: Portrait of a Mind*, p. xii.
12. *The New York Times*, August 25, 1974, Section 5, p. 4.
13. Blumenfeld, above, p. 140.
14. *The New York Times*, August 12, 1974, p. 23.
15. *The New York Times*, August 25, 1974, Section 5, p. 4.

16. *New York*, July 1, 1974, p. 34.
17. *Globe* (Boston), September 15, 1974, p. 6.
18. *The New York Times*, May 30, 1974, p. 35.
19. For example, the report of Philip Ben from Brussels, in *Maariv* (Tel Aviv), June 5, 1974.
20. *The New York Review of Books*, September 19, 1974, p. 29.
21. *Rolling Stone*, November 8, 1973, p. 40.

Chapter 4   Personal Success or National Interest

1. *The New York Times*, April 21, 1974, p. 1. Subsequent quotation in the same place.
2. *The New York Times Magazine*, December 29, 1974, p. 4.
3. *The New York Times*, August 12, 1974, p. 23.
4. *The New York Times*, August 20, 1974, p. 35.
5. *Globe* (Boston), September 15, 1974, p. 34.
6. *The Atlantic*, October, 1974, pp. 52, 59–60.
7. *Foreign Policy*, Summer, 1974, p. 68.
8. Thus William Şafire, in *The New York Times*, December 26, 1974, p. 37.
9. *The New York Times*, December 9, 1974, p. 35.
10. See especially the report by Seymour Hersh, in *The New York Times*, September 11, 1974.
11. *The New York Times*, October 13, 1974, p. 35.
12. *The New York Times*, August 27, 1974, p. 33.
13. *Present Tense*, Spring, 1974, p. 40.
14. *The New York Times*, April 21, 1974, p. 16.
15. *New York*, June 1, 1974.
16. Even as the Arabs retreated from large areas, at the height of the June War, the Soviet leadership expressed full confidence that they would sooner or later get America to force Israel to return them, according to the late Polish leader Gomulka, upon his return from an extraordinary meeting in Moscow of seven East European regimes, in *Tribuna Ludu* (Warsaw) of June 20, 1967.

Chapter 5   Sadat Waits

1. *The New York Post*, May 20, 1971, p. 31.
2. *Newsweek*, October 9, 1972, p. 116.
3. *The New York Post*, November 6, 1973, p. 34.

4. Thus, Seymour Maxwell Finger, who was Senior Advisor to the Permanent U. S. Representative to the U. N., in *Middle East Information Series*, February, 1972.
5. *Foreign Policy*, Spring, 1973.
6. *Bulletin of the American Academic Association for Peace in the Middle East*, January, 1973, p. 2.
7. *The New York Times*, August 29, 1974, p. 31.

Chapter 6   Tilting Toward Whom?

1. Ashman, who dwelled on Kissinger's career as a ladies' man, thought that his *modus operandi* was similar in his various endeavors. "The Kissinger approach to the military problem," he wrote, "was based on his standard come-on to a good-looking woman. Analyze, impress with your authority, bluff a little, work like hell, insist on winning, score, and move on!" (*Kissinger*, p. 96.)
2. *The New York Times*, September 25, 1973, p. 18.
3. *The New York Times*, September 26, 1973, p. 2.
4. *The New York Times*, September 21, 1973, p. 1, and September, 27, 1973, p. 16.
5. *Al-Anwar*, November 16, 1973.
6. As cited in *Newsweek*, October 29, 1973, p. 116.
7. Thus J. Bowyer Bell (author of *The Long War*) in his unpublished paper, "National Character and Military Strategy: The Egyptian Experience, October 1973," and Nadav Safran (author of *From War to War*) in *Foreign Affairs*, January, 1974, pp. 216–17.
8. *Time*, July 1, 1974, p. 33.
9. Leslie Gelb reported in *The New York Times* (June 23, 1974, p. 10) that "Kissinger and Schlesinger Deny Rift in October War."
10. *New York*, July 1, 1974, p. 37. Subsequent quotations from p. 33.
11. *The New York Post*, November 5, 1974, p. 5.
12. *Commentary*, September, 1974, p. 37. Subsequent quotations from pp. 37–38.
13. Palit, *Return to Sinai*, p. 139.

14. Ray Alan, in *The New Leader*, December 24, 1973, p. 8.
15. *The New York Times*, December 20, 1974, p. 7, and December 21, 1974, p. 9.

Chapter 7   Achievement vs. Ballyhoo

1. *The New York Review of Books*, September 19, 1974, p. 25.
2. *The New York Times*, September 24, 1974, p. 12.
3. Steel relates that, when the deal with the North Vietnamese appeared to founder on Thieu's obstinacy, Kissinger exploded in rage over what this would do to his *career* (above, p. 26).

Chapter 8   Who Wins, Who Loses

1. Thus Ronald Steel: "Although he is a superb negotiator—tactful, imaginative, indefatigable, and sensitive to nuance—his approach to politics is rigid and unimaginative. His talent is as a dealer, not as an innovator" (*The New York Review of Books*, September 19, 1974, p. 26).
2. For this information and the subsequent quotations, see Blumenfeld, *Henry Kissinger*, pp. 133–35.
3. *The New York Review of Books*, above, p. 25.
4. Holbrooke, *Globe*, (Boston) September 15, 1974, p. 34.
5. Above, p. 7.
6. *The New York Post*, June 6, 1974, p. 37.
7. Steel relates in the above (p. 27): "A lasting peace, 'Kissinger told the delegates to a conference on the Middle East the following year, is often an 'agonizing' task. He illustrated this with a revealing quotation:
   > 'Pain that cannot forget
   > falls drop by drop
   > upon the heart,
   > until in our despair
   > there comes wisdom,
   > through the awful
   > grace of God.' "
8. To foreign policy analysts in Washington, on March 21, 1974.
9. Tel Aviv's *Maariv* had reported these threats in detail (see *The New York Post*, May 10, 1974, p. 5). Earlier, Leslie Gelb reported in *The New York Times* (April 13, 1974, p. 2) direct

Kissinger pressure on Israel on Syrian disengagement, using the heavy burden of payment for American arms shipments to that country.

Chapter 9   Bases of (Mis)Information

1. *The New York Times*, August 6, 1974, p. 16.
2. *The National Observer*, December 29, 1973, p. 3.
3. *The New York Times*, June 8, 1974, p. 4.
4. *The New York Times*, December 14, 1973, p. 14.
5. *The New York Times*, December 11, 1973, p. 32.
6. *The New York Post*, November 8, 1973, p. 90.
7. Peter Grose, in *The New York Times*, May 21, 1974, p. 41.
8. November 29, 1973, p. 16.
9. June 20, 1973, emphasis added.
10. *Newsweek*, December 10, 1973, p. 56, emphasis added.
11. *The New York Times*, June 1, 1974, p. 8.
12. *The New York Times*, December 15, 1973, p. 13.
13. *The New York Times*, December 11, 1973, p. 9.
14. October 1, 1974, p. 30.
15. *Temperament and Character of the Arabs*, pp. 34–35.
16. *American Journal of Psychiatry*, February, 1972, p. 101.

Chapter 10   On the Spot

1. *Al-Ahram*, November 29, 1973. Subsequent quotations from the issue for October 23, 1973 and the same place.
2. *The New York Times*, November 29, 1973, p. 16.
3. *Al-Ahram*, December 29, 1967.
4. Cited in Samuel Merlin, *The Search for Peace in the Middle East*, pp. 91, 94.
5. *The Middle East and the West*, p. 125.
6. *Al-Ahram*, August 2, 1970.
7. *Journal of Palestine Studies* (Beirut), Autumn, 1971, pp. 6–7.
8. Thus, *Al-Ahram*, February 1, 1974.
9. Reported by the Israeli novelist Amos Oz, in *Crossroads*, July, 1972, p. 2.
10. Reported by a participant in a study mission of American editors, May 24–June 5, 1974.
11. Cited in *Brief* (Tel Aviv), January 1–15, 1974, p. 3.

Chapter 11   Do the Arabs Want Peace?

1. From the briefing of American editors by Major General Badri at the High War College in May of 1974.
2. *Brief*, April 1–15, 1974, p. 1.
3. From the stenographic record of one of the editors above.
4. *Middle East Intelligence Survey* (Tel Aviv), May 15, 1974, p. 29.
5. For example, on October 29, 1974, p. 1.
6. June 3, 1974, p. 13.
7. November 12, 1974, p. 15.
8. May 21, 1974, p. 10.
9. Henry Tanner, November 15, 1974, p. 17.
10. "Roundtable," WNET-TV (Newark), November 15, 1974.
11. *The New York Times*, November 15, 1974, p. 18.
12. *Brief*, February 16–28, 1974, p. 1.
13. *The New York Times*, November 4, 1974, p. 15.
14. Marvin Kalb revealed the State Department judgement, on CBS-TV Evening News on November 13, 1974. For the Ford statement, see *The New York Times*, November 15, 1974, p. 18.
15. *The New York Times*, October 21, 1974, p. 3. This thinking is widespread in the Arab world, as is also evident from Morton Kondracke's report from Beirut (*The New York Post*, December 10, 1974, pp. 4, 22), citing a Palestinian lawyer's view on the forthcoming change in America's position on the P. L. O.: "I look at it cynically. I do not think it is from any change of heart. I think it is just realistic for you to change attitude, in appreciation of the risks you face if you don't."
16. *The New York Times*, November 22, 1974, p. 6.
17. *The New York Times*, November 26, 1974, p. 46.

Chapter 12   How Much Will Israel Yield?

1. "Sixty Minutes," CBS-TV, March 10, 1974.
2. Cited in *Histadrut Foto News* (New York), May-June, 1974, p. 9.
3. *The New York Post*, November 9, 1973, p. 31.
4. *The New York Times*, August 15, 1974, p. 2.
5. *The New York Times*, September 15, 1974, Section 4, p. 5.
6. September 12, 1971, p. 31.
7. *Time*, December 10, 1973, p. 58.
8. *Yediot Achronot* (Tel Aviv), July 26, 1974.

Chapter 13 Russia, Influence and Oil

1. *The New York Times,* June 10, 1974, p. 6.
2. Terence Smith, August 18, 1974, Section 4, p. 4.
3. *The New York Times,* October 13, 1974, p. 35.
4. *The New York Times,* November 26, 1974, p. 1.
5. *The New York Times,* November 7, 1974, p. 7.
6. *The New York Times,* November 4, 1974, p. 15.
7. *The New York Times,* November 15, 1974, p. 17.
8. November 23, 1974, p. 30.
9. September 19, 1974, p. 42.
10. *The New York Times,* September 25, 1974, p. 3.
11. *Newsweek,* March 18, 1974, p. 52.
12. Jack Anderson, in *The Washington Post,* December 16, 1973, Section B, p. 7.
13. See especially, his article in *Foreign Affairs,* Winter 1972–73, and his essay in *The New York Times* of April 21, 1973.
14. Thus Deputy Assistant Secretary of State Rodger Davies, in a conversation with the writer on March 22, 1974.
15. *Platt's Oilgram News Service,* February 22, 1973.
16. In *The Washington Post,* above.
17. John Lee, in *The New York Times,* October 16, 1974, p. 59.
18. *The New York Post,* January 10, 1975, p. 39.
19. *The New York Post,* November 8, 1974, p. 43.
20. *The New York Times,* September 26, 1974, p. 29.
21. Jack Anderson in *The New York Post,* December 30, 1974, p. 31. And through James Reston, in *The New York Times,* December 6, 1974, p. 39.
22. *The New York Times,* April 28, 1974, Section 4, p. 21.
23. March 18, 1974, p. 52.
24. June 1, 1974, pp. 1, 8.
25. *The New York Times,* November 23, 1974, p. 3.
26. See the reports in *The Washington Post,* June 25, 1974, pp. 1, 9, and *The New York Times,* June 26, 1974, pp. 1, 4.
27. *The Washington Post,* June 26, 1974, p. 2.
28. *The New York Times,* November 15, 1974, p. 18.

Chapter 14 The Fate of the West

1. *Commentary,* January, 1958.
2. Joseph Kraft, *The New York Times Magazine,* November 7, 1971.

3. Bartley Crum, *Behind the Silken Courtain*, p. 249.

4. Marvin Kalb, CBS Radio (New York), May 2, 1971.

5. Graubard, *Kissinger*, p. 19. Subsequent quotation from p. 95.

6. *Congressional Record* for March 11, 1974.

7. *The New York Times*, December 3, 1974, p. 11, and December 4, 1974, p. 14.

8. *The New York Times*, November 27, 1974, p. 37.

9. *The New York Times*, December 9, 1974, p. 14, and December 10, 1974, p. 7.

10. *U. S. News & World Report*, November 25, 1974, p. 24.